CRASH COURSE
FOR THE SAT

CRASH COURSE
FOR THE SAT
The Last-Minute Guide to
Scoring High

Second Edition

by Jeff Rubenstein

Random House, Inc.
New York

www.PrincetonReview.com

Princeton Review Publishing
2315 Broadway
New York, NY 10024

E-mail: booksupport@review.com

Published in the United States by Random House, Inc., New York, and
simultaneously in Canada by Random House of Canada Limited, Toronto.

ISBN 0-375-76361-9

Editor: Allegra Burton
Designer: Stephanie Martin
Production Editor: Maria Dente
Production Coordinator: Jennifer Arias

Manufactured in the United States of America.

9   8   7   6   5   4   3   2   1

Second Edition

ACKNOWLEDGMENTS

Thanks to Faisel Alam, Karen Lurie, Andy Lutz, Evan Schnittman, and Rachel Warren for help and amusement.

Special thanks to Adam Robinson, who conceived of and perfected the Joe Bloggs approach to standardized tests, and many other techniques in this book.

CONTENTS

INTRODUCTION

WHAT IS THE SAT?

The SAT I: Reasoning Test—from now on, we'll just call it the SAT—is a three-hour, multiple-choice test used by many colleges as a factor in undergraduate admissions and placement decisions.

The SAT contains three scored Math sections, with a total of 60 questions. Two of the Math sections are 30 minutes each; the third is 15 minutes. The math questions appear in three different formats: five-choice problem solving questions, four-choice quantitative comparisons, and grid-ins. Quantitative comparisons ask you to compare two columns and determine which one is greater. Grid-ins are the only non–multiple-choice questions on the test; they ask you to find a numerical answer and mark it on a grid.

The SAT also contains three scored Verbal sections, with a total of 78 questions. Two of the Verbal sections are 30 minutes each; the third is 15 minutes. The two 30-minute sections consist of sentence completions, analogies, and critical reading; the 15-minute section consists only of critical reading questions.

The seventh section on the SAT is an unscored, experimental section, either Math or Verbal, which is used to test questions for future test administrations. There is no reliable way of knowing which of the seven sections is experimental, because the seven sections are randomly ordered.

How Important Is the SAT?

Unfortunately, your SAT score is often one of the most important pieces of your admissions portfolio. If your scores fall below a school's usual range, the admissions officers may look very critically at the other parts of your application; if your scores exceed the school's usual range, you will have a leg up on many others in the applicant pool. In general, smaller and more selective schools tend to place more weight on other factors such as your interview, your essays, and your extracurricular activities. On the other hand, larger schools (which have a very large applicant pool to choose from) tend to rely more heavily on SAT scores and high school grade point average. At these schools, admissions decisions may be based entirely (or almost entirely) on these two factors. This is not true, however, of every school; some schools have begun to de-emphasize the SAT, and a few have even made it optional.

WHAT IS THE PSAT?

The PSAT is a test that's very similar to the SAT. (In fact, the PSAT is usually composed of previously administered SAT questions.) It is given by most high schools to students in their junior (and occasionally sophomore) year. The PSAT is used to help select National Merit Scholars, but unless you're one of the very few who are in contention for these scholarships, it's really only a practice test. Colleges will not see your PSAT scores; only your high school will. But if you're interested in doing well on the PSAT, all the techniques that you will learn in this book apply just as well to the PSAT as they do to the SAT.

WHO WRITES THIS TEST, ANYWAY? WHAT WILL BE ON IT?

The SAT is written and administered by Educational Testing Service (ETS), under contract from the College Entrance Examination Board (better known as the "College Board"). The people who work at ETS are average folks who just happen to make a living writing tests. They aren't paid to care about students; they're paid to write and administer tests.

The Math sections of the SAT test only basic arithmetic, algebra, and geometry. But the questions are often confusingly worded, and ETS has planted plenty of trap choices to seduce you into picking incorrect answers. You may get the feeling at times that ETS has rigged the game against you—and you'd be right to feel that way. This book will review the basic math that you need to know, show you easier ways to solve the problems, and help you to avoid those traps.

The Verbal sections of the SAT test vocabulary and your ability to pick out facts from a reading passage. In this book, we'll help you improve your vocabulary and make the most of the vocabulary you already have. Moreover, we'll show you how to find facts in a passage efficiently with a technique that we've designed for the SAT.

I HEARD THIS TEST IS CHANGING, IS THAT TRUE?

Whereas this rumor is true, the changes will not take place until the spring of 2005. So don't start sweating just yet; most likely, you will narrowly miss the changes.

What are these changes, you might ask? Well, the biggest change is the addition of a 25-minute Essay and a 25-minute Grammar section, and the elimination of analogies and the quantitative comparisons. Also, ETS is going to expand the Reading Comprehension sections (hooray, right?) to include some "argument-style" questions.

How does this affect you? It means that ETS needs to start testing out how some of these new questions will be received by students taking the exam, so you might see a few odd ball or out-of-place questions that just don't fit the normal profile of an SAT question. So don't let your game slip if you see a strange question or two—you're probably in the Experimental section where ETS is trying out its new toys.

WHAT IS THE PRINCETON REVIEW?

The Princeton Review is the nation's fastest-growing test-preparation company. In just a few years, we've become one of the nation's leaders in SAT preparation primarily because our techniques work. We offer courses and private tutoring for all of the major standardized tests, and we publish a series of books on a variety of subjects. If you'd like more information about our programs or books, give us a call at 1-800-2-Review, or go online: www.PrincetonReview.com.

How to Use This Book

This book is divided into two parts. The first part covers the basic concepts and techniques you need to know to improve your score. It is divided into ten steps, each of which should take about an hour to cover. Each step will introduce some new material and present some "Your Turn" drills to reinforce that material. Because vocabulary is so important to the Verbal portion of the SAT, each step also includes a portion of The Princeton Review Hit Parade (the list of words that appear most frequently on the test).

The second part of the book is composed of some practice drills on which you can try out your newly acquired techniques. We suggest that you learn one step per day: read the technique chapters very carefully, do all of the "Your Turn" exercises, and learn the vocabulary for each step. If you still have time, try your hand at a few of the drills in the back of the book.

Because this book is a "crash course," it is intended to help you get the maximum improvement in a minimum amount of time. We won't waste your time going through every possible problem that might appear on the test. Rather, we'll teach you the essentials. If you have more time before the test, we also highly recommend that you purchase *10 Real SATs* (published by the College Board), which will allow you to take previously administered SATs under timed conditions.

TEN STEPS

In the first three Steps, we'll discuss some general strategies to help you get the best possible score on the SAT, and introduce some techniques that you can use on every part of the test. Some of our advice may sound a bit strange at first. You may even find yourself saying, "But my teacher would kill me if I did this on a test in school!" Just remember: This isn't school. Our techniques are specifically designed to get you points on the SAT—and they work.

STEP 1
DO THE RIGHT NUMBER
OF PROBLEMS

Most students think they need to do every problem on the SAT to get a great score, and they hurt their score because they try to do too many problems.

There are two reasons why it doesn't make sense to try every problem on the test. First, it's very hard to finish every question while maintaining a high level of accuracy. During timed tests, people naturally rush—and they make careless errors and lose points. Almost everyone is better off slowing down, using the whole time allowed to work on fewer problems, and answering more of those problems correctly.

You'll get a higher score if you do only 75 percent of the problems on this test and answer them correctly than if you do all of the problems and answer about half correctly. Likewise, you'll get a much higher score if you do only 50 percent of the problems on this test and answer them correctly than if you do three-quarters of them and only answer half correctly.

Here's how accuracy can help you: Let's say you answer 39 verbal questions correctly and 39 incorrectly. Roughly translated, you have earned 39 raw points for the right responses, but now you need to subtract out your "penalty" for the answers you got wrong. For every incorrect response, ETS subtracts $\frac{1}{4}$ of a point from your raw score. In our example, that works out to 10 points, which leaves you with a raw score of 29 (roughly a 470). Now, let's try a more accurate approach. If you answer only 45 questions and end up with 37 right and 8 wrong, you'll earn 37 raw points for the correct answers and a penalty of 2 points for the incorrect ones. After all that, you have 35 raw points (which is roughly a 500). In our second example, we left 33 questions blank, but ended up with a higher score! This is how you can hurt yourself by answering every question.

Second, not every question is of the same level of difficulty; in fact, most of the problems on this test are arranged in increasing order of difficulty within their sections: the earlier questions are easier, and they get gradually harder until the final questions are so difficult that only a small percentage of test takers answers them correctly. A hard question is worth no more than an easy question, so why waste time working on it?

WHICH PROBLEMS SHOULD I DO?

You should do the problems that are easiest for you. In general, the questions on the SAT are arranged in increasing order of difficulty.

Breakdown of Question Types in the Math Section

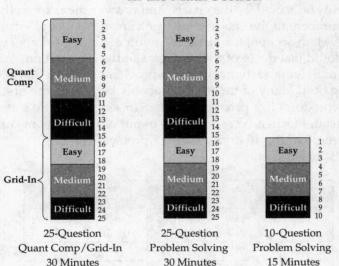

25-Question	25-Question	10-Question
Quant Comp/Grid-In	Problem Solving	Problem Solving
30 Minutes	30 Minutes	15 Minutes

Memorize this chart now. The most important question to ask yourself when you approach a problem on the SAT is: How difficult is it? If it's an easy question, go ahead and answer it. If it's a medium or hard question, be careful! Try to avoid solving these problems in the usual way. Instead, use one of our techniques, or try to take a good guess using Process of Elimination (POE), which you'll learn about in Step 2.

Learning to identify the easiest questions for you is *so* important that we've given all of the problems in this book the question number that they would have on an actual SAT.

Remember to always ask yourself: Is this question easy, medium, or hard? Should I do this problem, and if so, how should I approach it?

HOW MANY PROBLEMS SHOULD I DO?

Only the number of problems you need. You're much better off doing fewer problems and increasing your accuracy than doing too many problems and getting too few of them right.

The following charts show you how many problems you need to answer correctly in order to get a certain score. You should use all the time you're given to do only the number of problems indicated by the charts, and answer them correctly. (The numbers in the charts allow for a small margin of error.) On the Math section, for instance, if you're aiming for a 550, you should just do 16 of the problems in the 25-question Problem Solving section. Which 16 problems? The 16 that you like the best. Many of them will probably be among the first 16; but if you don't like problem number 15, skip it and do number 17 instead. Further, you should do 10 out of the 15 quant comp problems, 8 of the 10 grid-ins, and 7 problems on the 10-question section.

Math Scoring Chart				
Score	Prob Solv. (255–Q)	Quant Comp (15–Q)	Grid-Ins (10–Q)	Problem Solv. (10–Q)
400	7	5	4	4
450	12	7	4	4
500	14	9	6	5
550	16	10	8	7
600	20	12	8	8
650	23	12	9	9
700	All	14	All	All
750	All	All	All	All
800	All	All	All	All

Here's the chart for Verbal. If you're aiming for a 550, you need to answer a total of 44 problems correctly. Which 44? The ones that you like best. If you're strong in critical reading, maybe you'll try for 30 critical reading points, 7 analogies and 7 sentence completions. If you're weak in critical reading, you aim for 15 analogies, 15 sentence completions, and 14 critical reading questions. It's up to you. It's a good idea, though, to have a game plan in advance. Find one that plays to your strengths.

Verbal Scoring Chart	
Score	You Need
400	18
450	27
500	35
550	44
600	54
650	64
700	68
750	72
800	76

SET REASONABLE GOALS

If you're currently scoring 500, trying to score a 650 right away will only hurt you. Try to work your way up in easy stages. Pick a score range approximately 50 points higher than the range in which you're currently scoring. If you're currently scoring 500, aim for a 550; when you have reached 550, then you can aim for 600.

If you haven't ever taken a practice SAT, you can estimate your current SAT score by looking at your PSAT score. Add a zero to your PSAT score to see roughly what you would score on the SAT. For instance, if you scored a 50 Verbal and 55 Math on the PSAT, that corresponds to a 500 Verbal and 550 Math on the SAT.

SLOW DOWN.

Do fewer problems.

Answer more problems correctly.

Do the problems that are easiest for you.

Vocab Time

Turn to page 123 and memorize the Hit Parade Words for Step 1.

LEARN TO USE PROCESS
OF ELIMINATION

GUESS AGGRESSIVELY

Guessing aggressively basically means that if you can eliminate even one answer choice on a problem, you should take a guess.

You may have heard from various sources that the SAT has a guessing penalty, and that you shouldn't guess on the SAT. This is false. You should guess aggressively and often on the SAT. Here's why: To generate your final score, ETS first computes your raw score. ETS gives you one raw score point for every correct answer and subtracts $\frac{1}{4}$ of a raw score point for every wrong answer on your bubble sheet ($\frac{1}{3}$ of a point for quant comp). Blanks are not counted at all. This raw score is then converted to a scaled score on the 200–800 scale.

The SAT (or most of it, anyway) is a five-option, multiple-choice test. If you guess completely randomly on five questions in a row, you should—by random chance—get one of these five correct and four of them wrong. Because you'll get one point for the one correct answer, and lose a quarter of a point for each of the four wrong answers, your net raw score will be zero.

HINT

So, random guessing will not help or hurt you on the SAT. It simply counts for nothing.

So while it is true that you lose a fraction of a point for every incorrect answer on the test, this only has the effect of neutralizing completely random guessing. Guessing randomly has no effect on your score at all.

This means that you shouldn't waste your time by randomly guessing. However—and this is why you should guess aggressively and often—if you can eliminate even one choice and guess better than randomly, then guessing will increase your score. So you should get in the habit of guessing aggressively. Even if you can't get the correct answer, you should eliminate the choices you know are impossible or unreasonable, guess from the choices that remain, and move on to the next problem.

You don't have to know how to solve a problem in order to get the correct answer (or at least to be able to make a good guess). Aggressively using **Process of Elimination** (which we'll call **POE** from now on) will get you points on the SAT.

    1.   What is the capital of Malawi?

If you were to see this problem on the SAT (don't worry, you won't), you'd probably be stuck—not to mention a little upset. But the majority of the problems on the SAT don't look like the problem above. They look like the following:

    1.   What is the capital of Malawi?
       (A) Washington
       (B) Paris
       (C) Tokyo
       (D) London
       (E) Lilongwe

Not so bad anymore, is it? By knowing which choices must be wrong, you can often figure out what the answer is—even without knowing *why* it's the correct answer.

We will discuss POE for each problem type throughout the book, but there are two general principles of POE that you should learn right away: **Estimation** and **Joe Bloggs.**

ESTIMATION

On math problems, use common sense and estimate an answer before trying to solve. Often, several of the answers are unreasonable and can be eliminated right away. This will help you avoid careless mistakes and make a good guess, even if you can't solve the problem.

Read the following:

> 5. If 12 cans of food can feed 8 dogs for one
>   week, how many cans of food would be
>   needed to feed 6 dogs for two weeks?
>
>   (A) 9
>   (B) 12
>   (C) 16
>   (D) 18
>   (E) 24

Before you start to calculate, estimate. If 12 cans will feed 8
dogs for one week, and you want to know how many cans are
needed for two weeks, the answer must be larger than 12. So
eliminate (A) and (B). But six dogs are only being fed for two
weeks, so the answer must be less than 24. Eliminate (E). The
answer must be either (C) or (D). Now, if you can calculate the
answer, great. If not, you've got a 50 percent chance of a correct
guess.

You can estimate a lot more on the SAT than you might
think, particularly on geometry. Estimate whenever you can!

JOE BLOGGS

Suppose for a moment that you could look at the answers
recorded by the tester next to you (you can't). Also suppose
that you know for a fact that every one of your neighbor's
answers on the test is wrong. If, on problem 23, that person marked (C) as his or her answer, what would you do?
Eliminate choice (C), right?

Well, even though you can't look at your neighbor's page,
you can use this principle to get points on the test. We've cre-
ated an imaginary tester to accompany you during the exam, a
tester that we've named Joe Bloggs.

Now, Joe isn't stupid, he's just average. And when ETS
writes the SAT, they write it in a very particular way. They
write it so that Joe will get most of the easy problems correct,
some of the medium problems correct, and none of the hard
ones correct.

How do they do this? The test writers are very good at predicting what kinds of answer choices are attractive to the average person. They're good at it because they've been doing it for more than 40 years.

Joe Bloggs, the average test taker, always picks the answer that first attracts him. Choices that first attract him on math problems have nice round numbers that can be easily derived from other numbers in the problem. Choices that attract him on verbal problems have familiar words that remind him of words in the question.

Question Type	Joe Bloggs Selects	How Joe Does
Easy	What Seems Right	Mostly Right
Easy	What Seems Right	So-So
Easy	What Seems Right	All Wrong!

What does this mean for you? When you're working on easy problems, pick the choice that seems right to you. When you're working on medium problems, be careful. If you got the answer too quickly, check your work. Medium problems should take more work than easy problems. If you're working on a hard problem, eliminate the choices that first seem attractive; they are almost always traps.

Remember, though: Joe Bloggs gets the easy problems right. *Cross off Joe Bloggs answers only on the hard problems.* And don't forget: How do you know how hard a question is? By its question number.

Read the following example:

20. NEOLOGISM : LANGUAGE
    (A) rhetoric : speech
    (B) syllogism : grammar
    (C) innovation : technology
    (D) iconography : art
    (E) epistemology : philosophy

First, read at the question number. This is an analogy number 20, which means it's a hard analogy. You may not know what the word *neologism* means, but you (and Joe) know what *language* means. Because Joe likes to pick words that seem familiar and remind him of parts of the problem, which choices do you think he will pick? *Grammar* and *speech* remind Joe of *language*, so he will pick (A) or (B), which means that you should eliminate them. If you can't get any farther, guess from among (C), (D), and (E). In fact, the answer is (C).

Read this math problem:

25. Michelle rode her bicycle from her house to school at an average speed of 8 miles per hour. Later that day, she rode from school back home along the same route at an average speed of 12 miles per hour. If the round trip took her 1 hour, how many miles long is the round trip?

   (A) 8
   (B) $9\frac{3}{5}$
   (C) 10
   (D) $11\frac{1}{5}$
   (E) 12

Which choice do you think seems attractive to Joe at first? Because he sees the numbers 8 and 12 and the word "average," he will probably average 8 and 12 to get 10. Therefore, Joe will pick (C).

But now you know better. This problem is number 25, the hardest problem in the section. You know that Joe will get it wrong, so eliminate his choice, (C).

If Joe doesn't pick (C), what else might he pick? Either (A), 8, or (E), 12, because those are the numbers that appear in the problem. Cross them off as well. Then guess from either (B) or (D). (The answer is B. But we're not going to spend time on why.) If you can quickly cross off a few choices on a hard problem and make a good guess, you'll be in great shape.

HINT

Use POE and Joe Bloggs. They are your best friends on the SAT.

Guess Aggressively. If you can cross off even one answer choice, take a guess!

Vocab Time

Turn to pages 124-125 and memorize the Hit Parade Words for Step 2.

STEP 3

KNOW YOUR
DEFINITIONS—PART 1

The greatest number of errors on SAT Math actually occur in reading comprehension: test takers misunderstand what the question is asking for. Learn the following definitions well, and practice them on real problems.

THE BASICS PART I

Integers are numbers that have no fractional or decimal parts. Examples of integers are –10, –3, –2, –1, 0, 1, 2, 3, 10, 23, and 50. Zero is an integer. What kinds of numbers are not integers? 2.3, $\frac{1}{2}$, .6666, and so on.

Positive numbers are numbers that are larger than $\frac{1}{2}$ zero. Zero is **not** positive. Examples of positive numbers are, 1, 2.33, and 5.

Negative numbers are numbers that are less than zero. Zero is *not* negative. Examples of negative numbers are $-\frac{1}{2}$, –1, –2.33, and –5.

Even numbers are integers that can be divided by 2 with no remainder. Examples of even numbers are –4, –2, 0, 2, 4, and 6. Zero is even, even though it is neither positive nor negative!

Odd numbers are integers that cannot be divided by 2 evenly. Examples of odd numbers are –3, –1, 1, 3, 5, and 7.

Factors are the integers by which an integer can be divided with no remainder. The easiest way to find them is in pairs. For instance, 12 can be written as 1×12, 2×6, or 3×4. 12 can be divided by 1, 2, 3, 4, 6, and 12. These numbers are the factors of 12.

Multiples are the integers that can be divided by an integer. The easiest way to find multiples is to count up, adding the same number each time. $12 \times 1 = 12$; $12 \times 2 = 24$; $12 \times 3 = 36\ldots$. So, the first three positive multiples of 12 are 12, 24, and 36. But we can keep counting up by 12s forever: 12, 24, 36, 48, 60, 72, 84… *all* of these numbers are multiples of 12.

HINT

If you tend to confuse factors and multiples, remember this tip: Factors are Few, Multiples are Many. There are only a few factors for any given number, but there is always an infinite number of multiples!

Prime numbers are numbers that can be divided only by 1 and themselves. The first six prime numbers are 2, 3, 5, 7, 11, and 13. Zero and 1 are not prime, and 2 is the only even prime.

Distinct numbers are different numbers. For example, how many distinct numbers are there in the set {2, 5, 2, 6, 5, 7}? There are only four distinct numbers in this set: 2, 5, 6, and 7.

A digit is a figure from 0 through 9 that holds a place. For instance, the number 345.862 is composed of six digits. The digit 3 is in the *hundreds* place, the digit 4 is in the *tens* place, and the digit 5 is in the *units* place. The digit 8 is in the *tenths* place, the digit 6 is in the *hundredths* place, and the digit 2 is in the *thousandths* place.

Your Turn—Exercise 3.1

a. What are three consecutive odd integers whose sum is 15? _____

b. What are the factors of 10? _____

c. What are the prime factors of 10? _____

d. What are the factors of 36? _____

e. What are the prime factors of 36? _____

f. What are the first seven positive multiples of 6? _____

g. What are the first seven positive multiples of 4? _____

h. Numbers that are multiples of both 6 and 5 are also multiples of _____.

1. Which of the following does NOT have a remainder of 1?

 (A) $\dfrac{15}{7}$

 (B) $\dfrac{17}{8}$

 (C) $\dfrac{51}{3}$

 (D) $\dfrac{61}{4}$

 (E) $\dfrac{81}{10}$

2. Which of the following numbers has the digit 4 in the thousandths place?
 (A) 4000.0
 (B) 40.0
 (C) 0.4
 (D) 0.04
 (E) 0.004

3. Which of the following numbers is NOT prime?
 (A) 11
 (B) 23
 (C) 27
 (D) 29
 (E) 31

Answers to Exercise 3.1

a. 3, 5, 7

b. 1, 2, 5, 10

c. 2, 5

d. 1, 2, 3, 4, 6, 9, 12, 18, 36

e. 2, 3

f. 6, 12, 18, 24, 30, 36, 42

g. 4, 8, 12, 16, 20, 24, 28

h. 30

1. **C**   51 can be divided evenly by 3 with no remainder.

2. **E**   The thousandths place is the third to the right of the decimal.

3. **C**   27 can be divided by 3 and 9.

THE BASICS PART II

Consecutive numbers are numbers that are "in a row." 4, 5, 6 are consecutive integers; 6, 8, 10 are consecutive *even* integers.

Divisible means divisible with no remainder. 6 is divisible by 3, but 6 is not divisible by 5.

The **remainder** is what is left over after you divide. For example, when you divide 18 by 8, there is a remainder of 2.

A **sum** is the result of addition.

A **difference** is the result of subtraction.

A **product** is the result of multiplication.

Your Turn—Exercise 3.2

a. The product of two positive integers x and y is 30 and their sum is 11. What are x and y? _____

b. The product of two positive integers x and y is 30 and their difference is 13. What are x and y? _____

4. What is the least of three consecutive integers whose sum is 21?

(A) 4
(B) 5
(C) 6
(D) 7
(E) 8

5. If a, b, c, d, and e are consecutive even integers, and $a < b < c < d < e$, then $d + e$ is how much greater than $a + b$?

(A) 10
(B) 12
(C) 14
(D) 16
(E) 18

6. All numbers divisible by both 3 and 14 are also divisible by which of the following?

(A) 6
(B) 9
(C) 16
(D) 28
(E) 32

Answers to Exercise 3.2

a. 5 and 6

b. 15 and 2

4. **C**   The three consecutive integers must be 6, 7, and 8. The least of them is 6.

5. **B**   If the numbers are 2, 4, 6, 8, and 10, then 8 + 10 = 18 and 2 + 4 = 6. The last two numbers are 12 greater than the first two. (Don't forget that the numbers have to be consecutive and even!)

6. **A**   Look at the numbers that can be divided by 3 and 14. What is the first such number? 42. The only number in the answer choices that goes into 42 is 6.

ADVANCED ARITHMETIC—EXPONENTS AND SQUARE ROOTS

Exponents are easy to deal with, if you write them out. $3^3 = 3 \times 3 \times 3$. You can multiply and divide exponents that have the same base.

When you multiply, add the exponents: $3^4 \, 3 \times 3^3 = 3 \times 3 \times 3 \times 3 \, 3 \times 3 \times 3 \times 3 \times 3 \times 3 \times 3 \times 3 \times 3 = 3^7$

When you divide them, subtract the exponents.

$$\frac{3^4}{3^3} = \frac{3 \times 3 \times 3 \times 3}{3 \times 3 \times 3} = 3^1$$

If you raise an exponent to a power, multiply the exponents.

$$(3^2)^3 = 3 \times 3 \times 3 \times 3 \times 3 \times 3 \times 3 \times 3 \times 3 \times 3 \times 3 \times 3 = 3^6$$

Two special rules: •   Anything to the zero power is equal to 1: $3^0 = 1$

                     •   Anything to the first power is equal to itself: $3^1 = 3$

Finding a **square root** is just the opposite of raising a number to the second power. $\sqrt{4} = 2$, because $2^2 = 4$.

Square roots work just like exponents: You can always multiply and divide roots, but you can only add and subtract with the *same* root.

Multiplication and Division:

- $\sqrt{8} \times \sqrt{2} = \sqrt{16} = 4$
- $\sqrt{\dfrac{1}{4}} = \dfrac{\sqrt{1}}{\sqrt{4}} = \dfrac{1}{2}$
- $\sqrt{400} = \sqrt{400 \times 100} = \sqrt{4} \times \sqrt{100} = 2 \times 10 = 20$

Addition and Subtraction:

- $2\sqrt{2} + 3\sqrt{2} = 5\sqrt{2}$
- $4\sqrt{3} - \sqrt{3} = 3\sqrt{3}$
- $2\sqrt{3} + 3\sqrt{2}$ *cannot be added easily, because the terms do not have the same root.*

Your Turn—Exercise 3.3

a. $3^3 \times 3^2 = $ _____

b. $\dfrac{3^3}{3^2} = $ _____

c. $(3^3)^2 = $ _____

d. $x^6 \times x^2 = $ _____

e. $\dfrac{x^6}{x^2} = $ _____

f. $(x^6)^2 = $ _____

3. If $3^4 = 9^x$, then $x =$

    (A) 2

    (B) 3

    (C) 4

    (D) 5

    (E) 6

5. If $(3^x)^3 = 3^{15}$, what is the value of x?

    (A) 3

    (B) 5

    (C) 7

    (D) 9

    (E) 12

10. If $x^y \times x^6 = x^{54}$ and $(x^3)^z = x^9$, then $y + z =$

    (A) 10

    (B) 11

    (C) 48

    (D) 50

    (E) 51

Answers to Exercise 3.3

a. 3^5

b. 3^1

c. 3^6

d. x^8

e. x^4

f. x^{12}

3. **A**   If $3^4 = 9^x$, then $81 = 9^x$. Therefore, $x = 2$. You could also rewrite 3^4 as $3 \times 3 \times 3 \times 3 = 9 \times 9$.

5. **B**   If $(3^x)^3 = 3^{15}$, and you know that $x \times 3 = 15$, then $x = 5$.

10. **E**   Because $x^y \times x^6 = x^{54}$, y must be 48. Likewise, because $(x^3)^z = x^9$, z must be 3. Therefore, $y + z = 51$.

EASY ALGEBRA—SIMULTANEOUS EQUATIONS

Simultaneous equations are usually cumbersome, lengthy problems that require you to solve for one variable in terms of the other and then plug that into the other equation and solve for one of the variables. Confused? Well, don't be—on the SAT, simultaneous equations are easy! Just **Stack and Combine** the equations.

1.   If $2x - 3y = 7$ and $3x - 2y = 24$, what does $5x - 5y = ?$

Here's how to crack it

Don't try to solve for x or y individually—instead write them like this

$$\begin{array}{r} 2x - 3y = 7 \\ + \underline{3x - 2y = 24} \end{array}$$

Now if you add the equations, the problem becomes very simple!

$$\begin{array}{r} 2x - 3y = 7 \\ + \underline{3x - 2y = 24} \\ 5x - 5y = 31 \end{array}$$

So remember, if you have simultaneous equations, Stack and Combine. Sometimes you'll have to add the equations, and other times, you'll simply subtract one from the other. If you're not sure what to do, then add them—if it works, great, if not, then try subtracting.

Now try this one:

2.   If $6x - 7y = 13$ and $5x - 8y = -13$, what does $2x + 2y = ?$

Here's how to crack it

Again, if you try and solve for x or y, then you'll spend too much time doing this equation more than once. So stack 'em!

$$
\begin{array}{r}
6x - 7y = 13 \\
- \underline{5x - 8y = -13} \\
x + y = 26
\end{array}
$$

At this point, you have $x + y$, but you need $2x + 2y$. So multiply both sides by two!

$$2(x + y) = 2(26)$$

Therefore:

$$2x + 2y = 52$$

Vocab Time

Turn to pages 125-126 and memorize the Hit Parade Words for Step 3.

KNOW YOUR
DEFINITIONS—PART 2

AVERAGE, PERCENT, AND PERCENT CHANGE

Average (arithmetic mean) = $\dfrac{\text{total}}{\text{\# of things}}$. If you know any two of these parts, you can always solve for the third. If a student's test scores are 60, 65, and 75, the average score for those tests = $\dfrac{60+65+75}{3}$ = 66.67. If a student had an average score of 50 on three tests, the total score can be calculated, because the average (50) = $\dfrac{\text{total}}{3}$. Therefore his total score must have been 150.

Percent just means "divided by 100." So 20% = $\dfrac{20}{100} = \dfrac{1}{5} = 0.2$. Likewise, 8% = $\dfrac{8}{100} = \dfrac{2}{25} = 0.08$.

Any percent question can be translated into algebra—just use the following rules!

Word	Translates To
Percent	9 ÷ 100
Of	×
What	x (or any variable)
Is, Are, Equals	=

8 percent of 10	*becomes*	0.08 3 × 10 = 0.8
10 percent of 80	*becomes*	0.1 × 80 = 8
5 is what percent of 80?	*becomes*	$5 = \dfrac{x}{100} \times 80$
5 is 80 percent of what number?	*becomes*	$5 = \dfrac{80}{100} x$
What percent of 5 is 80?	*becomes*	$\dfrac{x}{100} \times 5 = 80$

Percent increase or percent decrease is always $\dfrac{\text{change}}{\text{original amount}}$.

If an $80 item is reduced to $60 during a sale, the percent decrease is the change in price ($20) over the original amount ($80), or 25%.

Your Turn—Exercise 4.1

a. If a student scores 70, 90, 95, and 105 on four tests, what is the average test score?

_____

b. If a student has an average score of 80 on four tests, what is the total of the scores received on those tests? _____

c. If a student has an average of 60 on tests whose totals add up to 360, how many tests has the student taken? _____

d. If the average of 4 and x is equal to the average of 2, 8, and x, what is the value of x?

_____

4. The average (arithmetic mean) of 4 numbers is 80. If two of the numbers are 50 and 60, what is the sum of the other two numbers?

_____

e. What percent of 5 is 6? _____

f. 60 percent of 90 is the same as 50 percent of what number? _____

14. A group of 30 adults and 20 children went to the beach. If 50 percent of the adults and 80 percent of the children went swimming, what percent of the group went swimming?

    (A) 30%
    (B) 46%
    (C) 50%
    (D) 62%
    (E) 65%

g. Jenny's salary increased from $30,000 to $33,000. By what percent did her salary increase? _____

h. In 1980, factory X produced 18,600 pieces. In 1981, factory X only produced 16,000 pieces. By approximately what percent did production decrease from 1980 to 1981? _____
_____

i. Jennifer took 6 tests and had an average score of 76 on those tests. If she takes two additional tests and receives a final average of 80 for all of her tests, what was her average on the two additional tests?
_____

Answers to Exercise 4.1

a. 90

b. 320

c. 6

d. $x = 8$

4. 210

e. 120%

f. 108

14. **D**   50% of the adults = 15, and 80% of the children = 16,
so 31 people total went swimming. 31 out of 50 is 62%.

g. 10%

h. $\dfrac{2,600}{18,600}$ = approximately 14% decrease.

i. 92

GEOMETRY DEFINITIONS

The **area of a square, rectangle,** or **parallelogram** is
length × *width*.

The **area of a triangle** is $\dfrac{1}{2}$ *base* × *height*.

The **area of a circle** with radius *r* is πr^2, so a circle with a radius
of 5 has an area of 25π.

The **perimeter** of any object is the sum of the lengths of its
sides. A triangle with sides 3, 4, and 5 has a perimeter of 12.

The **circumference** of a circle with radius *r* is $2\pi r$, so a circle
with a radius of 5 has a circumference of 10π.

The **slope** of a line is equal to $\dfrac{rise}{run}$. To find the slope, first take any
two points on the line and count off the perpendicular distance
you need to get from one of these points to the other, as follows:

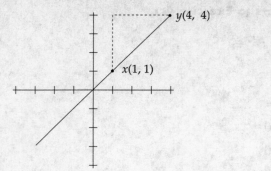

In the graph above, to get from point x to point y, we count up (rise) 3 points, and over (run) 3 points. So the slope is

$$\frac{\text{rise}}{\text{run}} = \frac{3}{3} = 1$$

No figure? No problem! If you need to find slope remember it's **rise** (the change in y- coordinates) over the **run** (the change in x-coordinates).

As a formula, slope $= (y_2 - y_1)/(x_2 - x_1)$.

Your Turn—Exercise 4.2

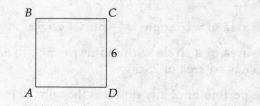

a.   What is the area of square $ABCD$ above?

_____

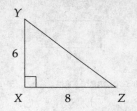

b.   What is the area of triangle *XYZ* above?
_____

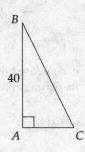

c.   If the area of triangle *ABC* is 400, what is
     its base?_____

d.   What is the area of the circle above with
     center *O*?_____

e.   What is its circumference? _____

f.   If *ABCD* is a rectangle, *x* = _____, and
     y = _____.

g.   What is the perimeter of rectangle *ABCD*?

h.   If the above figure is composed of two
     rectangles, what is its perimeter?

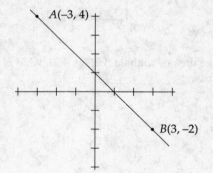

i   How many points do you count up (rise)
     to get from point *B* to point *A*?

j.   How many points must you count over
     (run) to get from point *B* to point *A*?

k.   What is the slope of the line above?

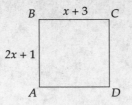

B $x + 3$ C

$2x + 1$

A   D

5. If *ABCD* is a square, what is its area?

(A) 2

(B) 3

(C) 5

(D) 20

(E) 25

Answers to Exercise 4.2

a. 36

b. 24

c. 20

d. 9π

e. 6π

f. 10, 5

g. 30

h. 22

i. 6

j. –6

k. –1

5. **E**

Vocab Time

Turn to pages 126 and 127 and memorize the Hit Parade Words for Step 4.

FAMILIARIZE YOURSELF WITH QUANTITATIVE COMPARISON AND GRID-INS

There are two question types on the SAT that you have probably never seen before (unless you've taken the PSAT or another standardized test). Just like the problem solving math questions, the quantitative comparison and grid-in problems cover basic arithmetic, algebra, and geometry. The questions in these sections are peculiar. Take a moment to look at what these problems ask you to do.

QUANTITATIVE COMPARISON: THE BASICS

Quantitative comparison (or **quant comp**) is exactly what it sounds like: Your job is to compare the two sides and determine which is larger.

Here are the rules:

Choose A if column A is always larger than column B

Choose B if column B is always larger than column A

Choose C if column A and column B are always equal

Choose D if you cannot tell which is larger—column A might be larger or column B might be larger

Notice that there are only four possible answers. *There is no choice (E) on quant comp.* So we suggest that you write A B C D in your test booklet to remind you of this as you work on the problem. Cross off letters as you eliminate them; this will make it easy to tell which choices are still possibilities.

One thing to note about quantitative comparisons is that an incorrect answer here has a $\frac{1}{3}$ point deduction. This is different from the rest of the test where $\frac{1}{4}$ of a point is deducted for an incorrect answer (except in grid-ins, where no points are taken off).

The most important rule for solving quant comp questions is: You don't always have to solve; you only have to compare.

Take a look at this problem:

Column A	Column B
1. $\dfrac{1}{2} + \dfrac{1}{3} + \dfrac{1}{11}$	$\dfrac{1}{2} + \dfrac{1}{4} + \dfrac{1}{11}$

In this case, each side has $\dfrac{1}{2}$ and $\dfrac{1}{11}$, so what you're really comparing is $\dfrac{1}{3}$ and $\dfrac{1}{4}$. Because $\dfrac{1}{3}$ is larger, the answer is (A). Try another:

Column A	Column B
12. The number of distinct prime factors of 36	The number of distinct prime factors of 28

How many distinct prime factors of 36 are there? Two of them (2 and 3). How many distinct prime factors of 28? Two, (2 and 7). So the answer is (C).

Your Turn—Exercise 5.1

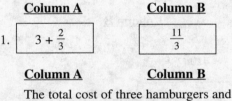

Column A	Column B
1. $3 + \dfrac{2}{3}$	$\dfrac{11}{3}$

Column A	Column B

The total cost of three hamburgers and two milkshakes is $2.40.

Column A	Column B
3. The cost of one hamburger	The cost of one milkshake

Column A	Column B

Square *ABCD* is inscribed in a circle.

	Column A	Column B
4.	The length of arc *ABC*	The length of arc *BCD*

Column A	Column B

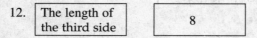

$$a^b = 8$$

a and *b* are integers.

	Column A	Column B
7.	*a*	*b*

Column A	Column B

Two of the sides of an isosceles triangle have lengths 3 and 8.

	Column A	Column B
12.	The length of the third side	8

Column A	Column B

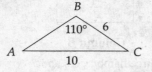

	Column A	Column B
13.	Area of triangle *ABC*	30

Answers to Exercise 5.1

1. **C** $3 + \dfrac{2}{3}$ is the same number as $\dfrac{11}{3}$.

3. **D**   Knowing the total of all five items does not allow us to solve for the individual price of any one of them. (You can think of this problem as an equation with two unknowns: $3h + 2m = \$2.40$.)

4. **C**   If a square is inscribed in a circle, all of its points are equally spaced on the circle. Therefore, the arcs have the same measure.

7. **D**   Variables a and b could be 2 and 3, because $2^3 = 8$. In this case, b would be larger than a. But a and b could also be 8 and 1, because $8^1 = 8$. In this case, a would be larger than b. So the answer must be (D).

12. **C**   Because an isosceles triangle has two equal sides, the two possibilities here are a triangle with sides 3, 8, and 8, or a triangle with sides 3, 8, and 3. But a triangle cannot have sides 3, 8, and 3. Try to draw one accurately, and you'll see why it doesn't work. (The rule you may remember from school is: The sum of any two sides of a triangle must be larger than the third side.) Therefore the triangle must have sides 3, 8, and 8. The third side must be 8, so the two columns are equal.

13. **B**   Because the base of ABC is 10, if the height were 6, then the area would be 30. But because side BC is 6, we know that the height of the triangle (which you can draw from point B down to line AC) must be less than 6. Therefore the area of ABC must be less than 30.

GRID-INS: THE BASICS

You will see ten questions on the SAT that ask you to bubble in a numerical answer on a grid rather than answer a multiple-choice question—these are **grid-in questions**.

Grid-ins are arranged in order of difficulty, and can be solved according to the methods already described for the multiple-choice problems on the test.

The only problem you might have with grid-ins is getting used to the way in which you are asked to answer the question. For each question, you'll have a grid like the following:

We recommend that you write the answer on top of the grid to help you bubble, but it's important to know that the scoring machine only reads the bubbles.

HINT

If you bubble incorrectly, the computer will mark the answer wrong.

THE BASIC RULES OF GRIDDING

If your answer (which will be a number) uses fewer than 4 boxes, you can grid it anywhere you like; you can grid an answer that needs 3 spaces in any of the 4 boxes, but to avoid confusion, we suggest that you start at the leftmost box.

You can grid your answer as either a fraction or a decimal if the fraction will fit.

You can grid an answer of .5 as either .5 or $\left[\frac{1}{2}\right]$.

You do not need to reduce your fractions if the fraction will fit.

If your answer is $\frac{2}{4}$, you can grid it as $\left[\frac{2}{4}\right]$, $\left[\frac{1}{2}\right]$, or .5

If you have a decimal that will not fit in the spaces provided, you must grid as many places as will fit.

If your answer is $\frac{1}{3}$, you can grid it as $\left[\frac{1}{3}\right]$, .333, but .33 is not acceptable.

You do not need to round your numbers, so we suggest that you don't.

You cannot grid mixed numbers. Convert all mixed numbers to ordinary fractions.

If your answer is $2\frac{1}{2}$, you must convert it to $\left[\frac{5}{2}\right]$ or 2.5

Try the Following Grid-Ins:

a. 125   b. $\frac{2}{12}$ c. $3\frac{1}{4}$ d. .8958

Answers to Grid-Ins

A 1 2 5

B 2 / 1 2

C 1 3 / 4

D • 8 9 5

(OR)

C 3 • 2 5

Your Turn—Exercise 5.2

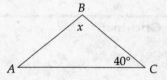

17. In triangle *ABC* above, if *AB = BC*, then *x =*

19. The sum of five consecutive integers, arranged in order from least to greatest, is 100. What is the sum of the next four consecutive integers?

20. If $5x^2 = 125$, what is the value of $5x^3$?

22. If 40 percent of 200 is equal to 300 percent of n, then n is equal to what number?

Answers to Exercise 5.2

17. Because the triangle is isosceles, with $AB = BC$, we know that angles A and C must have the same measure. So angle A must also be 40 degrees. Angles A and C have a combined measure of 80 degrees, and there are 180 total degrees in the triangle; x must measure $100°$.

19. If five consecutive integers have a sum of 100, they must be 18, 19, 20, 21, and 22. The next four consecutive integers are 23, 24, 25, and 26. Their sum is 98.

9	8		
	⊘	⊘	
⦿	⦿	⦿	⦿
	⓪	⓪	⓪
①	①	①	①
②	②	②	②
③	③	③	③
④	④	④	④
⑤	⑤	⑤	⑤
⑥	⑥	⑥	⑥
⑦	⑦	⑦	⑦
⑧	●	⑧	⑧
●	⑨	⑨	⑨

20. Because $5x^2 = 125$, we know that $x^2 = 25$ and $x = 5$. Therefore, $5x^3 = 5 \times 125 = 625$.

6	2	5	
	⊘	⊘	
⦿	⦿	⦿	⦿
	⓪	⓪	⓪
①	①	①	①
②	●	②	②
③	③	③	③
④	④	④	④
⑤	⑤	●	⑤
●	⑥	⑥	⑥
⑦	⑦	⑦	⑦
⑧	⑧	⑧	⑧
⑨	⑨	⑨	⑨

22. 40 percent of 200 is equal to $\frac{40}{100} \times 200 = 80$. So 80 is 300 percent of n. We can solve for n by translating this as $80 = \frac{300}{100} \times n$. So n must be $\frac{80}{3}$ or 26.667 (which you could grid either as 26.6 or 26.7).

2	6	.	6
	⊘	⊘	
⊙	⊙	●	⊙
	⓪	⓪	⓪
①	①	①	①
●	②	②	②
③	③	③	③
④	④	④	④
⑤	⑤	⑤	⑤
⑥	●	⑥	●
⑦	⑦	⑦	⑦
⑧	⑧	⑧	⑧
⑨	⑨	⑨	⑨

Vocab Time

Turn to page 127 and memorize the Hit Parade Words for Step 5.

STEP 6

PLUGGING IN

PLUGGING IN YOUR OWN NUMBERS

The problem with doing algebra is that it's very easy to make mistakes. Whenever you see a problem with variables in the answer choices, plug in. Start by picking a number for the variable in the problem (or for more than one variable, if necessary), solve the problem using that real number, and then see which answer choice gives you the correct answer.

Read the following problem:

2. If x is a positive integer, then 20 percent of $5x$ equals

   (A) x
   (B) $2x$
   (C) $5x$
   (D) $15x$
   (E) $20x$

Start by picking a number for x. Plug in a round number like 10. When you plug in 10 for x, change every x in the problem into a 10. Now the problem reads:

2. If 10 is a positive integer, then 20 percent of $5(10)$ equals

   (A) 10
   (B) $2(10)$
   (C) $5(10)$
   (D) $15(10)$
   (E) $20(10)$

Look how easy the problem becomes! Now you can solve: 20 percent of 50 is 10. Which answer is 10? (A).

Try it again:

8. If $-1 < x < 0$, then which of the following has the greatest value?

    (A) x

    (B) $2x$

    (C) x^3

    (D) $\frac{1}{x}$

    (E) $2x$

This time when you pick a number for x, you have to make sure that it is between -1 and 0, because that's what the problem dictates. So try $-\frac{1}{2}$. If we make every x in the problem, $-\frac{1}{2}$, the problem now reads:

8. If $-1 < -\frac{1}{2} < 0$, then which of the following has the greatest value?

    (A) $-\frac{1}{2}$

    (B) $\left(-\frac{1}{2}\right)^2 = \frac{1}{4}$

    (C) $\left(-\frac{1}{2}\right)^3 = -\frac{1}{8}$

    (D) $-\frac{1}{\frac{1}{2}} = -2$

    (E) $2\left(-\frac{1}{2}\right)^2 = -1$

Now you can solve the problem. Which has the greatest value? Choice (A) is $-\frac{1}{2}$, choice (B) equals $\frac{1}{4}$, choice (C) equals $-\frac{1}{8}$, choice (D) equals -2, and choice (E) equals -1. So choice (B) is the greatest.

Plugging In is such a great technique, that it makes even the hardest algebra problems easy. Anytime you can, plug in! Try one more:

9. The average of four consecutive multiples of 3 is *a*. What is the value of the largest of the numbers?
   (A) *a* + 6
   (B) *a* + 4.5
   (C) *a* + 3
   (D) *a* + 1.5
   (E) *a*

Here's how to crack it

Are there variables in the answer choices? Absolutely, so plug in! Pick 4 consecutive multiples of 3: for example, 3, 6, 9, and 12. What's the average of your multiples? Well, 3 + 6 + 9 + 12 = 30, divide that result by 4 and we have 7.5, which is our *a*. The question asks for the *largest* of the numbers, which, for the above example, is 12—circle it! This is your *target* value. Now, simply plug in *a* and see which answer works.

(A) 7.5 + 6 = 13.5   not 12, so cross it off!
(B) 7.5 + 4.5 = 12   BINGO! But check the other answers too!
(C) 7.5 + 3 = 10.5   not 12, so cross it off!
(D) 7.5 + 1.5 = 9   not 12, so cross it off!
(E) 7.5   not 12, so cross it off!

Easy, huh? Of course, because you made the algebra into simple arithmetic!

HINT
Whenever you see variables in the answer choices, PLUG IN!

What If There's No Variable?

Sometimes you'll see a problem that doesn't contain an x, y, or z, but a hidden variable. If your answers are percents or fractional parts of some unknown quantity (total number of marbles in a jar, total miles to travel in a trip), you can still try Plugging In a number.

Read this problem:

8. In a certain high school, the number of seniors is twice the number of juniors. If 60% of the senior class and 40% of the junior class attend the last football game of the season, what percent of the combined junior and senior class attends the game?

   (A) 60%
   (B) 53%
   (C) 50%
   (D) 47%
   (E) 40%

What number could you have that would make the math work on this problem incredibly easy? The number of students. So plug in a number and work the problem. Suppose that the number of seniors is 200 and the number of juniors 100.

If 60% of the 200 seniors and 40% of the 100 juniors go to the game, that makes 120 seniors and 40 juniors, or 160 students. What fraction of the combined class went to the game? $\frac{160}{300}$, or 53%. So the answer is (B).

Try this one:

9. Roger buys a pizza on Monday and eats $\frac{1}{5}$ that night. If on Tuesday, he packs $\frac{3}{5}$ of what's left of the pizza for lunch, what fraction of the original pizza is left in his refrigerator on Tuesday?

(A) $\frac{3}{25}$

(B) $\frac{1}{5}$

(C) $\frac{8}{25}$

(D) $\frac{11}{25}$

(E) $\frac{4}{5}$

Where's the hidden variable? What is the one quantity you don't know? The number of pieces or slices in a whole pizza. So plug in an easy number! Try 25 pieces (yes, Roger only purchases extra, extra large pizzas). How much did he eat on Monday? $\frac{1}{5}$ of 25, which works out to 5 pieces, so he must have 20 slices remaining. On Tuesday, he packs a lunch, which is $\frac{3}{5}$ of what's left, or $\frac{3}{5}$ of 20 slices, which is 12 slices. That leaves 8 slices in the fridge. Thus, the fractional part that is left in Roger's refrigerator is 8 slices out of 25 original or $\frac{8}{25}$. Answer (C).

PLUGGING IN ON QUANT COMP

Whenever you have variables on quant comp problems, plug in! The only difference is that on quant comp, you must plug in more than once.

First, try an ordinary number and see what answer you get. If you find that column A is larger, this doesn't prove that column A is *always* larger. But it does show you that (B) and (C) can't be right, and you can cross them off. Then you have a fifty-fifty chance if you need to guess. The answer must be (A) or (D).

Then, to see whether column A is always larger, try plugging in some different numbers to see if you can get a different answer to the problem. (It's especially helpful to try a few "weird" numbers such as 0, 1, negatives, and fractions.) If you can find a number with which column A is not always larger, then the answer to the problem is (D). If, however, you find that column A is always larger, then the answer is (A).

Likewise, if on your first plug-in, you find that column B is larger, you can eliminate (A) and (C), and the only possible choices are (B) and (D). If trying other numbers shows you that column B is always larger, then the answer is (B). If column B is not *always* larger, then the answer is (D).

If, on your first plug-in, you find that the two columns are equal, you can eliminate (A) and (B) and the answer must be (C) or (D). Try a different number to see if they are always equal. If they are, the answer is (C). If not, the answer is (D).

Take a look at the following problems:

Column A	**Column B**

$$-3 < z < 0$$

3.

$3 - z$	$z - 3$

Start by plugging in an easy number for z. Plug in –2, because z must be between –3 and 0. If z is –2, which column is larger? Column A is. So we can cross off (B) and (C). Now plug in again. You can't use 0 or 1 for z, so try a fraction. Suppose z is $-\frac{1}{2}$. Now which column is larger? Column A is still larger, so the answer is (A).

Now read the following problem from Exercise 5.1:

<u>**Column A**</u>　　　　<u>**Column B**</u>

a and *b* are integers.

$$a^b = 8$$

7.　| a |　　　| b |

Start by plugging in the obvious numbers for *a* and *b*. If *a* = 2 and *b* = 3, then $a^b = 8$. Which column is larger? Column B. But could we plug in different numbers and get a different answer? Yes. If *a* = 8 and *b* = 1, then $a^b = 8$. Now which column is larger? Column A, so the answer to this problem is (D).

Your Turn—Exercise 6.1

4.　On Tuesday, Martha does $\frac{1}{2}$ of her weekly homework. On Wednesday, she does $\frac{1}{3}$ of the remaining homework. After Wednesday, what fractional part of her homework remains to be done?

(A) $\frac{1}{6}$

(B) $\frac{1}{5}$

(C) $\frac{1}{4}$

(D) $\frac{1}{3}$

(E) $\frac{1}{2}$

14. If $a = \frac{b}{c^2}$ and $c \neq \frac{1}{b^2}$, then $\frac{1}{b^2} =$

(A) ac^2

(B) $a^2 c^4$

(C) $\frac{1}{ac^2}$

(D) $\frac{1}{a^2 c^4}$

(E) $\frac{a^2}{c^4}$

17. If $p \neq 0$, then $\dfrac{\frac{1}{8}}{2p} =$

(A) $\frac{1}{4p}$

(B) $\frac{p}{4}$

(C) $\frac{4}{p}$

(D) $\frac{4p}{3}$

(E) $4p$

Column A	**Column B**
	$ab = 0$

2. a 0

4.   **Column A**   **Column B**

$$x - y^2 > 0$$
$$x^2 - y > 0$$

x	y

Answers to Exercise 6.1

4. **D**   Plug in a number for the amount of homework Martha has. Say she has 12 pages of work to do. If she does half of this on Tuesday, she does 6 pages, and there are 6 pages left. If on Wednesday, she does one-third of the remaining 6 pages, that means she does 2 more pages. So she has 4 pages remaining of the original 12. What fractional part is left over? $\frac{4}{12}$, or $\frac{1}{3}$.

14. **D**   Pick numbers for a, b, and c such that $a = \frac{b}{c^2}$. You can pick $4 = \frac{16}{2^2}$. Now the question becomes: what is $\frac{1}{b^2}$ or $\frac{1}{16^2}$. The answer is $\frac{1}{256}$. Plug your numbers into each answer choice. Which choice works out to be $\frac{1}{256}$? Choice (D).

17. **B**   Pick a number for p. How about 2? Now the problem reads $\frac{\frac{1}{8}}{2(2)}$ and the answer is $\frac{1}{2}$. Plug your numbers into each answer choice—which one says $\frac{1}{2}$? (B) does.

2. **D**   For the first plug-in, plug in 0 for a and 5 for b. This makes it true that $ab = 0$. Which column is larger? They're equal. So we can cross off (A) and (B). Now, can you plug in different numbers that will give a different answer? Plug in 5 for a and 0 for b. This still makes it true that $ab = 0$. But this time, column A is larger than column B, so the answer is (D).

4. **A** For the first plug-in, pick easy numbers like 5 and 2 for *x* and *y*, respectively. You can eliminate answer choices (B) and (C) because *x* was greater than *y*. Next, try plugging in some weird numbers. Negative numbers won't work, nor will fractions, because both will violate the restrictions. Try 1 and 0 for *x* and *y*. Again, column A is greater, so it must be the answer.

PLUGGING IN THE ANSWER CHOICES

You can also plug in when the answers to a problem are actual values, such as 2, 4, 10, or 20. Why would you want to do a lot of complicated algebra to solve a problem when the answer is right there on the page? All you have to do is figure out which choice it is.

How can you tell which is the correct answer? Try every choice until you find the one that works. Even if this means you have to try all five choices, Plugging In is still a relatively fast and reliable means of getting the right answer.

But if you use your head, you almost never have to try all five choices. When you plug in the answer choices, begin with choice (C), the middle number. If choice (C) works, you're done. If choice (C) doesn't work because it's too small, try one of the larger numbers. If choice (C) doesn't work because it's too big, try one of the smaller numbers. You can almost always find the answer in two or three tries.

Do the following problem:

4. If the average (arithmetic mean) of 8 and *x* is equal to the average of 5, 9, and *x*, what is the value of *x*?

   (A) 1
   (B) 2
   (C) 4
   (D) 8
   (E) 10

Start with choice (C) and plug in 4 for x. The problem now reads:

4. If the average (arithmetic mean) of 8 and 4 is equal to the average of 5, 9, and 4 . . .

Does this work? Is the average of 8 and 4 equal to the average of 5, 9, and 4? Yes. Therefore (C) is the answer. Neat, huh?
Try one more:

10. If $(x - 2)^2 = 2x - 1$, which of the following is a possible value of x?

    (A) 1
    (B) 2
    (C) 3
    (D) 6
    (E) 7

If you try plugging in (C), 3, for x, the equation becomes $1 = 5$, which is false. So (C) can't be right. If you're not sure which way to go next, just pick a direction, and try the choices. It won't take very long to figure out the correct answer. If we try plugging in (B), 2, for x, the equation becomes $0 = 3$, which is false. If we try plugging in (A), 1, for x, the equation becomes $1 = 1$, which is true, so the answer is (A).

Your Turn—Exercise 6.2

8. If $3^{x+2} = 243$, what is the value of x?

    (A) 1
    (B) 2
    (C) 3
    (D) 4
    (E) 5

14. If $\frac{24x}{4} + \frac{1}{x} = 5$, then $x =$

(A) $-\frac{1}{6}$

(B) $\frac{1}{6}$

(C) $\frac{1}{4}$

(D) $\frac{1}{2}$

(E) 2

Answers to Exercise 6.2

8. **C**   Begin by plugging in the middle number, 3, for x. Is $3^5 = 243$? Yes, and the answer is (C).

14. **D**   If you try plugging in (C) $\frac{1}{4}$ for x, the equation becomes $\frac{6}{4} + 4 = 5$, which is false. If you try plugging in (D), $\frac{1}{2}$ for x, the equation becomes $\frac{12}{4} + 2 = 5$, which is true.

Vocab Time

Turn to pages 128 and 129 and memorize the Hit Parade Words for Step 6.

STEP 7

WHAT ELSE DO I KNOW?: GEOMETRY

Now that you've learned the basic geometry definitions from Step 4, you're ready to tackle more complex geometry problems.

Geometry problems on the SAT are not hard because the rules of geometry are difficult; there are only a few rules, and most of them will be printed in your test booklet. (The formulas for the area of a circle, square, and triangle can be found on the first page of every Math section.) So what makes the geometry difficult on the SAT? It's that ETS doesn't simply ask you to use a formula. You almost always have to use more than one rule to solve a problem, and it's often difficult to know which rule to use first.

HINT

Whenever you see a diagram, ask yourself: What else do I know? Write everything you can think of on your booklet.

You may not see right away why it's important, but write it down anyway. Chances are good that you will be making progress toward finding the answer without even knowing it.

Here's a classic example:

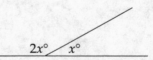

3. In the figure above, what is the value of x?

    (A) 30
    (B) 40
    (C) 50
    (D) 60
    (E) 80

It may not be obvious to you how you should go about solving this problem. But what do you know about this diagram? You see a line, and we know that the angles on a line always add up to 180. Write that on your diagram.

Now you can see that whatever x is, the sum of angles marked $2x$ and x must equal 180. So we can write the equation $2x + x = 180$, which equals $3x = 180$, so $x = 60$. The answer is (D). (You also could have plugged in the answer choices).

Try this again with the following problem:

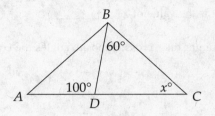

13. In triangle ABC above, $x =$

    (A) 30
    (B) 40
    (C) 50
    (D) 60
    (E) 70

Notice that you don't know what angle A and angle B are. What do you know? You know that a straight line is 180 degrees, so given that angle ADB is 100 degrees, angle CDB must be 80 degrees. Knowing that angle CDB is 80, and that DBC is 60, you can figure out that angle DCB must be 40, because $80 + 60 + 40 = 180$. The answer is (B), 40.

Your Turn—Exercise 7.1

(The sum of the angles that make up every line is 180 degrees.)

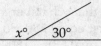

a.   What is the sum of 30° and x? _____

b.   What is the value of x? _____

(When two straight lines cross, opposite angles are equal.)

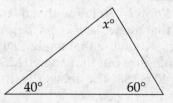

c.   What is the value of x? _____
     y? _____ z? _____

(The sum of the angles inside every triangle is 180 degrees.)

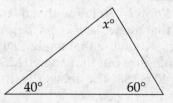

d.   What is the sum of 60, 40, and x?

     _____

e.   What is the value of x? _____

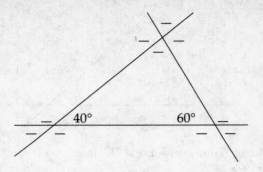

f. What are all of the angles on the above diagram?

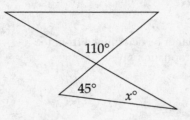

4. In the figure above, what is the value of x?

(A) 25

(B) 30

(C) 35

(D) 40

(E) 50

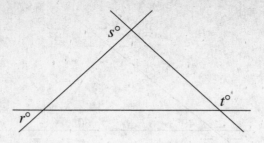

5. In the figure above, if $r = 75°$, then
   $r° + s° + t° = ?$

   (A) 25°
   (B) 105°
   (C) 255°
   (D) 330°
   (E) cannot be determined from the
       information given

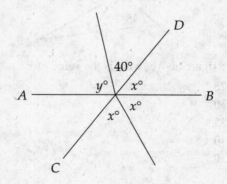

6. In the figure above, if *AB* and *CD* are
   lines, what is the value of *y*?

   (A) 60
   (B) 70
   (C) 75
   (D) 80
   (E) 85

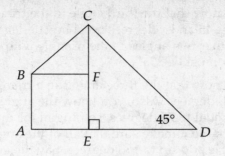

13. If the area of square *ABFE* = 25 and the
    area of triangle *BCF* = 10, what is the
    length of *ED*?

    (A) 7
    (B) 8
    (C) 9
    (D) 10
    (E) 14

Answers to Exercise 7.1

a. 180

b. 150

c. $x = 135, y = 45, z = 135$

d. 180

e. 80

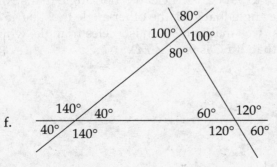

f.

4. **A**   You know that the third angle in the triangle with angles 45 and x degrees must be 110 degrees. Because the other two angles in the triangle with x are 45 and 110, x must be 25.

5. **D**   You know that the three angles in a triangle add up to 180 degrees. Also, you know the angle opposite to r is equal to 75 degrees, so plug in for the remaining angles—just make sure that all of the angles in the triangle add up to 180 degrees. Say the angle adjacent to s is 5 degrees and the angle adjacent to t is 100 degrees (remember, you're just making up your own numbers). That means that angle s becomes 175 degrees (with that 5-degree angle you plugged in, it forms a straight line) and angle t becomes 80 degrees. If you add up $r + s + t$, it adds up to 330 degrees, or answer (D). Don't believe us? Try Plugging In some different numbers—it'll always add up to 330 degrees!

6. **D**   You know that the three angles labeled x are on a straight line, and therefore must add up to 180. Because $3x = 180$, $x = 60$. Because the angles x, 40, and y must add up to 180, and you know that $x = 60$, $60 + 40 + y = 180$, and $y = 80$.

13. **C**   If the area of the square $ABFE$ is 25, then each of its sides must be 5. Because BF is 5, and the area of triangle BCF is 20, then side CF must be 4, making EC equal to 9. Because ECD has one angle that's 90 and one angle that's 45, the other angle must be 45 degrees. This makes ECD an isosceles triangle, which means that, if EC is 9, so is ED.

Vocab Time

Turn to page 129 and memorize the Hit Parade Words for Step 7.

In the next few chapters, we'll discuss some methods to help improve your score on the Verbal sections of the SAT. Many of these questions test your vocabulary, but even if you don't know every word, aggressive use of POE and smart guessing can help you make the most out of the vocabulary that you know.

STEP 8

SPEAK FOR YOURSELF: SENTENCE COMPLETIONS

WHAT IS A SENTENCE COMPLETION QUESTION?

Here are the instructions as you will see them on the SAT:

Each sentence below has one or two blanks, each blank indicating that something has been omitted. Beneath the sentence are five words or sets of words labeled A through E. Choose the word or set of words that, when inserted in the sentence, best fits the meaning of the sentence as a whole.

Example:

Medieval kingdoms did not become constitutional republics overnight; on the contrary, the change was ————.

(A) unpopular
(B) unexpected
(C) advantageous
(D) sufficient
(E) gradual

Most students try to solve sentence completion questions by rereading the sentence five times, trying a different word in the blank each time, and hoping to find the one that sounds right. This is not only a waste of time (why would you want to read the sentence five times?) but it's also unhelpful; all of the choices will probably sound equally bad. Moreover, the correct answer on a sentence completion question is not correct because of how it sounds, but because of what it means.

SPEAK FOR YOURSELF

The way to solve a sentence completion question is to try putting your own word in the blank. If you can't think of the exact word, think of what kind of word should go in the blank. Is it a positive word? A negative word? An active or passive word? Only then should you look at the answer choices and pick the word that's closest to the word that you chose.

If you find yourself tempted to read the answer choices first, cover them up with your hand. Force yourself to figure out what the word in the blank should mean. How can you do that?

YOU'RE SMARTER THAN YOU THINK

Try this exercise: In the following sentence, what word do you think should go in the blank?

1. Susan was ————— when the formula, which had worked just yesterday, failed to produce the expected result.

What word did you put in the blank? "perplexed"? "confused"? Something of this sort has to be the word in the blank. How about this one:

2. Although she was never considered pretty as a child, Margaret grew up to be a ————— adult.

What word did you put in the blank? "beautiful"? "pretty"? "lovely"? Here you can figure out what the word in the blank has to mean, without looking at the answer choices.

Try it once more:

3. Once a cheerful person, the years of fruitless struggle against government waste made him a very————— man.

Even if you couldn't figure out the exact word that went in the blank, you probably figured out that it had to be a word that's fairly close in meaning to "unhappy" or "bitter." That will be good enough to get the right answer, or at least to get a very good guess at the right answer.

This is why you should always approach sentence completion questions by speaking for yourself.

THE CLUE AND TRIGGER WORDS

To help you speak for yourself, learn to look for the clue and trigger words.

The Clue

How did you know what word went in the blank in the above sentences? There are always clues in the sentence that tell you what the word is supposed to mean.

Reread the first example:

> 1. Susan was ———— when the formula, which had worked just yesterday, failed to produce the expected result.

How did you know that the word had to be something like "perplexed"? Because there is a clue: "failed to produce the expected result." This tells us how Susan must feel.

Every sentence has some clue in it. Look for the clue, and it will help you determine the word that goes in the blank.

Trigger Words

Other important tools you have at your disposal are trigger words. These are words in the sentence that tell you how the word in the blank relates to the clue. For instance, look at the second sentence you tried:

> 2. Although she was never considered pretty as a child, Margaret grew up to be a ———— adult.

How did you know that the word in the blank had to be a word like "beautiful"? Because the word "although" told you that there was a contrast in the sentence: she was never considered pretty as a child, but she *was* a pretty adult.

There are also trigger words that indicate that the word in the blank has the same meaning as the clue. For instance:

> 4. Because Susan could not stand Jim's boorish manners, she ———— to be near him at parties.

In this case, what sort of word goes in the blank? The trigger word *because* tells you that the word in the blank will go along with the clue "could not stand Jim's boorish manners." The word in the blank must therefore be something like "hated" or "despised."

The most common **same-direction trigger words** are *and*, *because*, and *in fact*, and the colon (:) and semi-colon (;) also act as same-direction triggers.

The most **common opposite-direction trigger words** are *but, yet, although, nevertheless, however, once, in spite of,* and *despite*. When you see these words, the word in the blank will usually mean the opposite of the clue.

When trying to find the right word for the blank, always look for the clue and trigger words. They will tell you what sort of word you need.

Here are a few sentence completion problems from which we've removed the answer choices. (You can find the complete problems with answer choices on the next page.) Read the sentence, and put your own word in the blank. Then look on the next page and see which word comes closest to the word you picked.

1. Many feature films are criticized for their ——— content, even though television news is more often the medium that depicts violent events in excessive detail.

6. In a vitriolic message to his troops, General Patton insisted that he would ——— no further insubordination, no matter how barbarous the ensuing engagements might become.

7. Chang realized that she had been ——— in her duties; had she been more vigilant, the disaster may well have been avoided.

1. Many feature films are criticized for their ———— content, even though television news is more often the medium that depicts violent events in excessive detail.

   (A) discretionary
   (B) graphic
   (C) dramatic
   (D) artistic
   (E) honest

The clue in this sentence is "even though television news is more often the medium that depicts violent events." The word in the blank should mean something like "violent." The closest word in the choices is (B).

6. In a vitriolic message to his troops, General Patton insisted that he would ———— no further insubordination, no matter how barbarous the ensuing engagements might become.

   (A) impede
   (B) brief
   (C) denote
   (D) brook
   (E) expose

The clue here is "no further insubordination, no matter how." Did you pick a word like "tolerate" or "stand for" in this case? That's exactly the meaning of the word in the blank. The words in the choices are hard, but eliminate what you can and take a good guess. The answer is (D).

7. Chang realized that she had been ———
    in her duties; had she been more vigilant,
    the disaster may well have been avoided.

    (A) unparalleled
    (B) irreproachable
    (C) derelict
    (D) arbitrary
    (E) punctual

The clue in this sentence is "had she been more vigilant."
The word in the blank must mean the opposite of vigilant. The
closest choice is (C).

TWO BLANKS: TWICE AS EASY

Some of the sentence completion questions will have two
blanks rather than just one. To solve these questions, do them
one blank at a time. Pick one blank or the other, whichever
seems easier to you, and figure out what word should go in
the blank. (Often, but not always, the second blank is easier to
figure out.) Then cross off all of the choices that don't work for
that blank.

   If more than one choice remains, pick a word for the other
blank and see which of the remaining choices works best.
   Read this example:

2. The scientific community was ———
    when a living specimen of the coelacanth,
    which they feared had been ———, was
    discovered by deep-sea fishermen.

    (A) perplexed . . common
    (B) overjoyed . . dangerous
    (C) unconcerned . . exterminated
    (D) astounded . . extinct
    (E) dismayed . . alive

The clue for the second blank is that a living specimen was found, which the scientists feared was ————. So the second blank must mean something like "destroyed." Only choices (C) and (D) are possible, so you can eliminate the others. Now look at the first blank. How did the scientists feel about the discovery? They were probably happy about it. Of (C) and (D), which choice works with the first blank? Choice (D).

SENTENCE COMPLETION SUMMARY

1. Think of your own word to fit in the blank.

2. To help you figure out the meaning of the blank, look for clues in the sentence and pay close attention to trigger words.

3. If you can't think of a precise word for the blank, at least think of what kind of word should go there. Is it a positive word? A negative word? An active or passive word?

4. On two-blank questions, do one blank at a time.

Your turn—Exercise 8.1

1. After the dinner, Bob sat around and _____ _____ the new tax laws passed by Congress; he was upset and let everyone know it.

   (A) exemplified
   (B) condemned
   (C) propagated
   (D) construed
   (E) proliferated

2. Once it was revealed that Milli Vanilli had not sung the songs on their album, their _____ time in the spotlight became even more fleeting.

    (A) sustained
    (B) glamorous
    (C) ephemeral
    (D) infamous
    (E) lucid

3. The employees joked that their manager was _____; even when they were deriding him in his presence, he seemed _____ and unbothered.

    (A) coy . . garrulous
    (B) gregarious . . reticent
    (C) inept . . stoic
    (D) nonplussed . . oblivious
    (E) pernicious . . charmed

4. Shockingly _____ conditions exist in many of the villagers' homes, which lack electricity and indoor plumbing.

    (A) wonderful
    (B) primitive
    (C) advanced
    (D) vibrant
    (E) mellifluous

5. Surprisingly, Gina was _____ to seeing the action movie, despite having professed an avid _____ for the genre.

   (A) amenable . . aversion
   (B) opposed . . antipathy
   (C) perplexed . . joy
   (D) convinced . . elation
   (E) agreeable . . pleasure

6. Madeline was always even-tempered; all of her friends were often amazed by her _____ in pressure-filled situations.

   (A) equanimity
   (B) belligerence
   (C) penitence
   (D) exquisiteness
   (E) silence

7. Blake was consistently _____ and concise, choosing to speak with fewer words than his colleagues.

   (A) verbose
   (B) obsolete
   (C) tenuous
   (D) intrepid
   (E) laconic

Answers to Exercise 8.1

1. **B**   *Criticized* is a good word for the blank, because Bob was *upset about the new tax laws.* *Condemned* is closest in meaning to *criticized.*

2. **C**   According to the sentence, their career became even more *fleeting.* So recycle what they've given you, and put *fleeting* in the blank. Only ephemeral means this.

3. **D**   Do the second blank first. The boss was not bothered by his employees' derision, therefore he must've been *unbothered.* Eliminate (A). Now look at the first blank; if his employees made fun of him to his face, they must joke around that he's *clueless.* Thus (D) is the best answer.

4. **B**   Houses that lack indoor plumbing or electricity are operating in the Stone Age. Therefore, shockingly *bad* or *primitive* conditions prevail. Pick (B).

5. **A**   First, notice the trigger in the sentence: *despite* denotes a change of direction. Thus, the first blank is different from the second. The only answer choice that contains words that are in opposite directions is (A).

6. **A**   How is Madeline in high-pressure situations? Well she's always *even-tempered,* so recycle this clue. The only word that means *even-tempered* is *equanimity,* or (A).

7. **E** Blake is *concise* and uses very few words.
        So put *not talkative* in the blank. Which
        word means this? (E) *laconic*. If you
        didn't know that, then eliminate those
        words which you know do not mean
        concise and take a guess. Otherwise,
        study your vocabulary!

Vocab Time

Turn to page 130 and memorize the Hit Parade Words for Step 8.

Step 9

Make a Sentence:
Analogies

WHAT IS AN ANALOGY?

Here are the directions as you will see them on the SAT:

Each question below consists of a related pair of words or phrases, followed by five pairs of words or phrases labeled A through E. Select the pair that best expresses a relationship similar to that expressed in the original pair.

Example:

CRUMB : BREAD
(A) ounce : unit
(B) splinter : wood
(C) water : bucket
(D) twine : rope
(E) cream: butter

An **analogy question** asks you to determine the relationship between the two capitalized words, and then to choose the pair of words that has the same relationship. In the above example, a crumb is a piece of bread, and a splinter is a piece of wood. Therefore, the answer is (B).

IF YOU KNOW BOTH WORDS

The best way to figure out the relationship between the two capitalized words is to make a defining sentence using the two words. What's a defining sentence? A defining sentence is a sentence that starts with one of the words, and then goes on to define that word in terms of the other. When possible, use the word "is" or "means" to link the two words. For instance, take the analogy APPLE : FRUIT. A defining sentence would be "an apple is a kind of fruit" or "the word 'apple' means a kind of fruit." Then all you have to do is try the same sentence with each of the answer choices, and see which one works best.

Here's the complete problem:

10. APPLE : FRUIT
    (A) meal : restaurant
    (B) macaroni : cheese
    (C) dessert : vegetable
    (D) beef : meat
    (E) crust : pizza

Now read the choices using our sentence:

(A) is a *meal* a kind of *restaurant*? No.

(B) is *macaroni* a kind of *cheese*? Nope.

(C) is *dessert* a kind of *vegetable*? Definitely not.

(D) is *beef* a kind of *meat*? Yes. This could be correct.

(E) is *crust* a kind of *pizza*? No.

So the best answer is (D). It's the only choice that works with the sentence we made to define *apple* and *fruit*.

Now try a different analogy:

10. COMPANY : PRESIDENT
    (A) team : athlete
    (B) hospital : patient
    (C) airline : passenger
    (D) library : reader
    (E) army : general

You may find it easier in this case to write your sentence in reverse: "A president is the leader of a company." That's fine—just be sure to read the answer choices in reverse as well. Now read the choices using the same sentence:

(A) is an *athlete* the leader of a *team*? Maybe.

(B) is a *patient* the leader of a *hospital*? Definitely not.

(C) is a *passenger* the leader of an *airline*? No.

(D) is a *reader* the leader of a *library*? No.

(E) is a *general* the leader of an *army*? Yes. This is a possible choice.

Which of these choices seems the best? (A) is possible, but it's not as good as we'd like. An athlete might be the leader of a team, but the right word for the leader of a team is "coach." (E) has the strongest relationship, and is the best answer.

TIPS FOR MAKING GOOD SENTENCES

Making a sentence is the best way to solve analogies. To make your job easier, here are a few guidelines:

- Make your sentence as brief and straightforward as possible. Keep it simple!

- Begin your sentence with one of the capitalized words, followed by the word "is" or "means," and end the sentence with the other capitalized word.

- Try to maintain the words exactly as they are written. For instance, don't change "FIGHT" into "FIGHTING." You may find that it takes some practice to learn to make up good sentences this way, but it's well worth the effort.

Make Up a More Precise Sentence

Sometimes the first sentence you make up for an analogy isn't sufficient to get the right answer. Take a look at the following example:

HELMET : CYCLIST
- (A) baseball : catcher
- (B) badge : sheriff
- (C) goggles : welder
- (D) brush : painter
- (E) shoe : runner

Say that the first sentence that you made was "a helmet is worn by a cyclist." Check all five answer choices.

(A) is a *baseball* worn by a *catcher*? No. Eliminate this choice.

(B) is a *badge* worn by a *sheriff*? Yes.

(C) are *goggles* worn by a *welder*? Yes.

(D) is a *brush* worn by a *painter*? No. Eliminate this choice.

(E) is a *shoe* worn by a *runner*? Yes.

We only eliminated two choices using our original sentence. Now what? Make a slightly more precise sentence. Keep the original sentence, but add one more detail to it. In this case, why does a cyclist wear a helmet? For protection. So our new sentence will be: "A helmet is worn by a cyclist for protection." Now check the three choices that are left.

(A) [already eliminated]

(B) is a *badge* worn by a *sheriff* for protection? No.

(C) are *goggles* worn by a *welder* for protection? Yes.

(D) [already eliminated]

(E) is a *shoe* worn by a *runner* for protection? No.

So the best answer is (C). Easy, right?

Recycled Relationships
A few relationships appear over and over on the SAT. Learn them!

PART OF/KIND OF/MEMBER OF

PETAL : FLOWER

BAT : MAMMAL

ACTOR : CAST

A *petal* is part of a *flower*. A bat is a kind of *mammal*. An actor is a member of a *cast*.

DEGREE (LARGER/SMALLER DEGREE OF)

BREEZE : GALE

FAMISHED : HUNGRY

ARID : DRY

A *gale* is a strong *breeze*. Famished means very *hungry*. *Arid* means very *dry*.

FUNCTION (USED TO/SERVES TO)

ORNAMENT : ADORN

SCISSORS : CUT

BUTTRESS : SUPPORT

An *ornament* is something used to *adorn*. *Scissors* are used to *cut*. A *buttress* serves to *support*.

WITHOUT/LACK OF

AMORPHOUS : FORM

NAÏVE : SOPHISTICATION

JUVENILE : MATURITY

Amorphous means *without form*. *Naïve* means without *sophistication*. Something or someone that's *juvenile* is lacking in *maturity*.

Your Turn—Exercise 9.1

Practice making sentences from the following word pairs:

GIGANTIC : LARGE _____

FADE : BRILLIANCE_____

DICTIONARY : WORDS_____

ADHESIVE : BIND_____

LETTERS : ALPHABET_____

ETERNAL : END_____

COTTAGE : HOUSE_____

VERSE : POEM_____

SYLLABUS : COURSE_____

ANTISEPTIC : SANITIZE_____

ZOOLOGIST : ANIMALS_____

DISHONESTY : LIAR_____

CALORIMETER : ENERGY_____

JURY : TRIAL_____

RECLAMATION : LAND_____

VACUOUS : EMPTY_____

Answers to Exercise 9.1

Gigantic means very *large*.

Fade means to lose *brilliance*.

A *dictionary* contains *words*.

An *adhesive* is used to *bind*.

The *alphabet* is made up of *letters*.

Eternal means without *end*.

A *cottage* is a type of *house*.

A *verse* is a part of a *poem*.

A *syllabus* is the plan for a *course*.

An *antiseptic* is used to *sanitize*.

A *zoologist* studies *animals*.

Dishonesty is a characteristic of a *liar*.

A *calorimeter* is an instrument used to measure *energy*.

A *jury* decides the outcome of a *trial*.

Reclamation is the process of making *land* reusable.

Vacuous means to be extremely *empty*.

Try the Following Analogies:

11. MANSION : HOUSE
    (A) novelist : writer
    (B) leaf : tree
    (C) boulder : rock
    (D) desert : sand
    (E) engine : automobile

12. HAMMER : CARPENTER

    (A) bread : baker

    (B) brush : painter

    (C) gun : farmer

    (D) courtroom : juror

    (E) secret : criminal

20. METEOROLOGY : WEATHER

    (A) philology : love

    (B) epistemology : disease

    (C) physiology : mind

    (D) demography : population

    (E) astrology : planets

11. **C**   A *mansion* is a large *house*, and a *boulder* is a large *rock*.

12. **B**   A *hamme*r is a tool used by a *carpenter*, and a *brush* is a tool used by a *painter*.

20. **D**   *Meteorology* is the study of *weather*, and *demography* is the study of *population*.

IF YOU DON'T KNOW BOTH WORDS

If you don't know the capitalized words, or don't know them well enough to make a sentence, you can still get the correct answer (or at least a very good guess) by using Process of Elimination. There are two important ways to use POE on analogies: Working Backward and Side of the Fence.

Working Backward

The first step to **Working Backward** is to look at the five answer choices one at a time. For each choice, ask yourself: Do these words have a clear relation? Many of the wrong answer choices will contain unrelated words. If the words in an answer choice have no clear relation, then they cannot possibly be the correct answer on an analogy question.

How do you determine if a pair of words has a relation? Try to make a defining sentence with them. If you know the words, but can't make a good sentence with them, then it's likely that they have no relation.

Some of the pairs may sound like they go well together, like "salt : pepper" or "push : fight." But can you really make a good sentence that defines one of these words in terms of the other? Is salt a kind of pepper? A very big pepper? No. These words have no direct relationship.

The same happens for "push : fight." You certainly might push someone in a fight, but is "fight" really part of the meaning of the word "push"? Does a "push" mean an action that starts a fight? Does a fight always involve a push? It might seem like these words go well together, but they have no definite relation.

If a pair of words is unrelated, cross it off. It can't be the answer to an analogy. If you really have to stretch to make a good sentence, then it's likely that the words are only weakly related, and you should avoid that choice.

Further, if you can find a relation between the words in an answer choice, but you know that the capitalized words don't have the same relation, you can cross that choice off.

Your Turn—Exercise 9.2
Decide which of the following pairs have a clear relation by making sentences with them. If you think a pair of words has no relation, put an "X" next to that pair. If you don't know the words well enough to tell whether they are related, leave it blank.

TADPOLE : FROG _____

SOPORIFIC : SLEEP _____

PREDICTED : DISASTER_____

SOLITARY : CONVICTION _____

BIAS : PREJUDICED _____

ENLARGE : PICTURE _____

RESOLUTE : DETERMINED_____

VERIFIABLE : DEBATE _____

VAGUE : CLARITY _____

HARDEN : SHAPE _____

INTEGRITY : MOTION _____

STUBBORN : INJURY _____

Answers to Exercise 9.2

A *tadpole* is a young *frog.*

Soporific means causing *sleep.*

(no relation)

(no relation)

Prejudiced means having a *bias.*

(no relation)

Resolute means very *determined.*

(no relation)

Vague means lacking in *clarity.*

(no relation)

(no relation)

(no relation)

Side of the Fence

If you don't know the capitalized words well enough to make a sentence with them, but you have some sense of their relationship, try to figure out if the two words are on the "same side of the fence" or on "opposite sides of the fence." If the words are similar in meaning, then the correct answer choice must also contain words that are similar in meaning. If the words are opposites, then the correct answer choice will be a pair of opposites. Take, for instance, the following problem:

20. THERMAL : HEAT
    (A) pure : polluted
    (B) parched : moisture
    (C) fictional : character
    (D) terrestrial : land
    (E) loyal : traitor

You may have trouble making a sentence with the words *thermal* and *heat*. But you probably know that they are very close in meaning. The correct answer choice must also have a pair of words close in meaning. So we can cross off any words that have no relationship, or that are opposites. How about (A)? *Pure* and *polluted* are opposites. So are *loyal* and *traitor*. The words in (C) don't really have a clear relation. If you don't know the words in (B) or (D), leave them both in, and take a guess. (In fact, the answer is (D).)

Try one more:

21. ENLIGHTEN : IGNORANT
    (A) insist : successful
    (B) abridge : concise
    (C) free : constrained
    (D) insult : complimentary
    (E) cure : healthy

This is a tough analogy. If you find it difficult to make a sentence with the words *enlighten* and *ignorant*, try **Side of the Fence**. Are these words similar or opposite in meaning? Opposite. So check the answer choices. The correct answer must also be a pair of opposites. The only real opposites here are choices (C) and (D). If you can't get any farther, you've still got a fifty percent chance of answering this question correctly. (By the way, the answer was (C). To *enlighten* means to make someone less *ignorant*. To *free* someone means to make that person less *constrained*.)

Your Turn—Exercise 9.3

Are the following words similar or opposite?

ASTONISH : SURPRISE _____

OUTCAST : POPULARITY _____

EVIL : MALEFACTOR _____

CARICATURE : PORTRAIT _____

EXPERIENCED : NAÏVE _____

FUNNY : HILARIOUS _____

ANARCHIST : AUTHORITY_____

ESOTERIC : COMPREHEND _____

HUMID : MOISTURE _____

EXTEMPORANEOUS : PREPARATION_____

DELIBERATE : FORETHOUGHT_____

Answers to Exercise 9.3

Similar (*astonish* means to *surprise* a great deal)

Opposite (an *outcast* lacks *popularity*)

Similar (a *malefactor* intends/does *evil*)

Similar (a *caricature* is an exaggerated *portrait*)

Opposite (an *experienced* person is not *naïve*)

Similar (*hilarious* means very *funny*)

Opposite (an *anarchist* rejects all forms of *authority*)

Opposite (something *esoteric* is difficult to *comprehend*)

Similar (*humid* means the presence of a great deal of *moisture*)

Opposite (*extemporaneous* means without *preparation*)

Similar (something *deliberate* is performed with *forethought*)

Your Turn—Exercise 9.4

Now try the following analogies. They range from medium to difficult, so if you can't make a good sentence, use Working Backward and Side of the Fence to make a good guess. For more analogies drills, see page 171.

15. ENRAGED : ANGRY
    (A) ecstatic : happy
    (B) juvenile : nonchalant
    (C) dangerous : enticing
    (D) taciturn : verbose
    (E) jealous : greedy

18. HOT : SCALDING
    (A) proud : sophisticated
    (B) modest : tactful
    (C) surprising : shocking
    (D) strange : habitual
    (E) trivial : important

20. CHASTISE : CRITICIZE

    (A) exculpate : accuse
    (B) intensify : placate
    (C) alert : liberate
    (D) rebuke : rebuff
    (E) doubt : gainsay

21. MEDLEY : SONGS

    (A) ring : romance
    (B) oven : bread
    (C) collage : photographs
    (D) plug : outlet
    (E) badge : rank

22. MULISH : COMPLY

    (A) abstemious : indulge
    (B) chalk : board
    (C) servile : follow
    (D) prodigal : wasteful
    (E) callous : harden

23. SMIRK : SATISFACTION

    (A) applause : happiness
    (B) glower : anger
    (C) sweat : exhaustion
    (D) gasp : surprise
    (E) shiver : fear

Answers to Exercise 9.4

15. **A**   *Enraged* means very *angry*. If you aren't sure of the meaning of the words, you probably know that they are similar in meaning. The words in choices (B) and (C) have no clear relation and can be eliminated. The words in choice (D) are opposite in meaning. The best choice is (A), because *ecstatic* means very *happy*.

18. **C**   *Scalding* means very *hot*. Again, even if you can't make a defining sentence with the two words, they are very similar in meaning. Choices (A) and (D) have no clear relation, and the words in choice (E) are opposite in meaning. Because *shocking* means very *surprising*, the best choice is (C).

20. **D**   To *chastise* means to *criticize* very severely. These words are similar in meaning, so you can eliminate choices (A) and (B), which are opposites. Choices (C) and (E) have no clear relation, so the best choice is (D).

21. **C**   A *medley* is a collection of *songs*. Because (B) and (D) have no relation, eliminate them. And (A) and (E) don't work with our sentence.

22. **A**   *Mulish* means unwilling to *comply*. If you don't know the relationship between the words, go directly to the answer choices. Answers (B) and (E) don't make any sense when you work backward. Because *abstemious* means unwilling to *indulge*, it's the best answer.

23. **B**   A *smirk* is a sign of *satisfaction*. (A) and (C) aren't related so eliminate them. (B), (D), and (E) all have the same relationship, so make your sentence more specific: a *smirk* is a facial expression of *satisfaction*. Now only (B) works.

ANALOGIES SUMMARY

1. If you know both of the capitalized words, make a defining sentence. See which choices fit that sentence. Start with the most simple, straightforward sentence possible. If necessary, make the sentence more precise until you find the choice that is the best match.

2. If you don't know one of the capitalized words, Work Backward.

   a. See which choices have good relationships by making defining sentences for the words in the answer choices. If you are sure that the words in a given answer choice have no relation, eliminate that choice.

   b. For each answer choice for which you can make a sentence, Work Backward to see if that sentence could work with the capitalized words. If not, eliminate that choice.

   c. If you don't know whether the words in a choice are related, leave it in. It could be right.

3. If you can't make a sentence, but you think that the two words are related, use Side of the Fence. If the capitalized words are similar, the correct answer will contain similar words. If the capitalized words are opposite, the correct answer must be a pair of opposites.

Vocab Time
Turn to page 132 and memorize the Hit Parade Words for Step 9.

STEP 10

TREASURE HUNT: CRITICAL READING

WHAT IS CRITICAL READING?

Here are the directions as you will see them on the test:

> The passage below is followed by questions based on its content. Answer the questions on the basis of what is stated or implied in the passage and in any introductory material that may be provided.

You might think that this means that you need to read the passage carefully, understand it thoroughly, or make complex inferences from the information contained in the passage. You don't.

Think of critical reading as a treasure hunt: All the answers to the questions are buried somewhere in the passage. All you've got to do is find them.

The passages will usually be a mix of science, social science, humanities, and narrative passages. On any given section, you might see one long passage, two shorter passages, or a "dual passage." If you have two shorter passages and you feel short on time, pick the one with which you feel more comfortable.

APPROACHING CRITICAL READING

The problem with **critical reading questions** is, of course, that these passages are boring, dense, brutish, and long. How can you get the most points in the least amount of time, and in the most reliable way? Well, not by reading the whole passage carefully. You can do it by knowing where to find the answers quickly, and then finding the choice that restates what is said in the passage.

An Encyclopedia

If someone were to give you a ten-volume encyclopedia and ask you the year of Pasteur's death, would you begin reading at the *A*s and work all the way through to the *P*s until you found Pasteur? Of course not. You'd go right to the entry on Pasteur and read only the five or six lines that you need. That's how you should approach critical reading questions.

Your Treasure Hunt

So here are the steps to finding your answers in the most efficient way:

1. Read the "blurb" (the introductory material).

2. Go to the questions. Do the specific questions first and the general questions later.

3. Put the question in your own words.

4. Find the answer to the question in the passage.

5. Pick the answer choice that comes closest to what you found in the passage.

SPECIFIC QUESTIONS

Almost every question on Critical Reading will be a **specific question**. That is, it will ask you for facts from particular parts of the passage. Some questions give you a specific line number, some give you a key concept (what we call "lead words"), and some ask you for the definition of a word.

To answer any specific question, the method is the same. Hunt for the answer in the passage using the clues in the question, read that area of the passage to find the answer to the question, and then pick the answer choice that is the best paraphrase of what the passage says.

The most common kinds of specific questions are **line number, lead word,** and **vocabulary in context questions**:

- **Line number questions**: If the question gives you a line reference, go back to the passage and read that line in context (from about five lines before the line reference, to five lines following the line reference). Then, find the choice that restates what is said in these lines.

- **Lead word questions**: If the question only gives you a lead word (such as "What does the author feel about Type II Levers?" or "It can be inferred from the author's discussion of Type II Levers, that . . ."), then skim through the passage until you find the point at which that concept (Type II Levers) is discussed. Reread these lines, and then find the answer choice that paraphrases the information in these lines.

- **Vocabulary in context:** If the question asks you to define a word, treat the question like sentence completions. Go back to the sentence in which the word occurs and cross it out. Then, read the sentence and pick your own word to put in its place. This will give you an idea of what the word should mean. (Be careful, because the word in question may not have the meaning that's most familiar to you!) Then, look for the choice that best states what you think the word means in context.

POE on Specific Questions

There are two important rules of thumb on specific questions:

Whenever you see a diagram, ask yourself: What else do I know? Write everything you can think of on your booklet.

- Avoid extremes
- Avoid offense

ETS does not pick extreme or offensive passages for its tests. If you see a choice that's very extreme (extreme choices sometimes use words such as *must*, *always*, *only*, *every*) or potentially very offensive to a certain class of people, eliminate it.

Here are some examples of choices that you can eliminate:

- judges deliberately undermine the constitution
- doctors are the only people who can cure malaria
- it was entirely misleading
- disparage the narrow-mindedness of modern research
- all his beliefs about his parents were wrong

Likewise, for questions that ask you about the author's attitude or tone, eliminate extremes, such as:

- sarcasm
- ridicule
- repugnance
- condemnation

GENERAL QUESTIONS

You may see one or two **general questions** that ask you for the main point or primary purpose of the passage. Save these for last; after answering the specific questions, you'll almost always have a good sense of the main idea. If you're stuck, try rereading the first and last lines of every paragraph, and any line that contains a trigger word (*but, yet, although, nevertheless, however*). These are the most important lines in the passage, and you will most likely find the main idea in these lines.

POE on General Questions

The two biggest pitfalls to avoid on general questions are:

- too specific
- impossible to accomplish

Choices that are discussed only in one part of the passage are too specific to be the main point. The main point of a passage is something that relates to the passage as a whole. Also, use common sense: Any choice that is impossible to accomplish in a couple of paragraphs (such as "prove that comets killed the dinosaurs") can't be the answer to a general question.

DUAL PASSAGE

One section of the SAT will probably contain a "dual passage," that is, two passages that have differing viewpoints on a common theme. Following the passages will be some questions that are relevant to only one passage or the other, and some questions that ask you to compare the two passages. These comparison questions are usually harder, so the best strategy is:

1. Read the blurb for Passage 1.

2. Answer the questions on Passage 1.

3. Read the blurb for Passage 2.

4. Answer the questions on Passage 2.

5. Answer any questions that ask you to compare the two passages.

This way, you'll save the hardest problems for last—and if you run out of time, you can skip them entirely.

Try these techniques on the following passage:

John Dewey was an American educator and thinker. In the following excerpt from Democracy and Education, *he explains why education is necessary for human beings.*

The most notable distinction between living and inanimate things is that the former maintain themselves by renewal. A stone when struck resists. If its resistance is greater than the force of the blow struck,
5 it remains outwardly unchanged. Otherwise, it is shattered into smaller bits. Never does the stone attempt to react in such a way that it may maintain itself against the blow, much less so as to render the blow a contributing factor to its own continued action. While
10 the living thing may easily be crushed by superior force, it nonetheless tries to turn the energies that act upon it into means of its own further existence. If it cannot do so, it does not just split into smaller pieces (at least in the higher forms of life), but loses its iden-
15 tity as a living thing. As long as it endures, the living thing struggles to use surrounding energies in its own behalf. It uses light, air, moisture, and the material of soil. Life is a self-renewing process through action upon the environment.

20 With the renewal of physical existence goes, in the
case of human beings, the recreation of beliefs, ideals, hopes, happiness, misery, and practices. The
continuity of any experience, through renewing of the
social group, is a literal fact. Education, in its broadest
25 sense, is the means of this social continuity of life.
Every one of the constituent elements of a social
group, in a modern city as in a savage tribe, is born
immature, helpless, without language, beliefs, ideas,
or social standards. Each individual, each unit who is
30 the carrier of the life-experience of his group, in time
passes away. Yet the life of the group goes on.

The primary ineluctable facts of the birth and death
of each one of the constituent members in a social
group determine the necessity of education. Even in a
35 savage tribe, the achievements of adults are far beyond
what the immature members would be capable of if
left to themselves. With the growth of civilization, the
gap between the original capacities of the immature
and the standards and customs of the elders increases.
40 Mere physical growing up, mere mastery of the bare
necessities of subsistence will not suffice to repro-
duce the life of the group. Deliberate effort and the
taking of thoughtful pains are required. Beings who
are born not only unaware of, but quite indifferent
45 to, the aims and habits of the social group have to be
rendered cognizant of them and actively interested.
Education, and education alone, spans the gap.

Society exists through a process of transmission quite
similar to biological life. Without this communication
50 of ideals, hopes, expectations, standards, opinions,
from those members of society who are passing out
of the group life to those who are coming into it,
social life could not survive. If the members who
compose a society lived on continuously, they might
55 educate the new-born members, but it would be a task

directed by personal interest rather than social need.
Now it is a work of necessity. If a plague carried off
the members of a society all at once, it is obvious
that the group would be permanently done for. Yet
60   the death of each of its constituent members is as certain as if an epidemic took them all at once. But the
graded difference in age, the fact that some are born
as some die, makes possible through transmission
of ideas and practices the constant reweaving of the
65   social fabric. Yet this renewal is not automatic. Unless
pains are taken to see that genuine and thorough
transmission takes place, the most civilized group will
relapse into barbarism and then into savagery.

1.   The author discusses a stone (lines 3–9) in
     order to explain
     (A) the forces necessary to destroy rock
     (B) the difference between living and
          non-living beings
     (C) why living things cannot be split into
          pieces
     (D) why living things are easier to crush
          than stones
     (E) the nutritional requirements for life

The stone is an example that illustrates something. What
does it illustrate? Read about five lines above (in this case,
from the beginning of the passage) to about five lines below
the example, and look for the idea supported by the case of the
stone. The answer is in the first line: the "distinction between
living and inanimate things is that the former maintain themselves by renewal." Which choice paraphrases this line?
(B) does.

2. The primary purpose of the passage is to

   (A) argue that we should spend more money on public schools

   (B) explain why the author wants to be a teacher

   (C) prove that humans would die without education

   (D) recount the author's own experience as a student

   (E) support the claim that good education is essential for human beings

Because this is a general question, save it for last. Not only is the blurb a good clue to the main point, but notice that many of the questions revolve around the question of education. Choice (A) might be something that the author believes, but public schools are never mentioned in the passage. Choice (C) is simply too big a task to be accomplished in a short passage. Choices (B) and (D) are too personal; the author never discusses his own memories or wishes. The best choice is (E).

3. The word "ineluctable" as used in line 32 most nearly means

   (A) unhappy

   (B) absurd

   (C) unchangeable

   (D) indifferent

   (E) proven

Cross off the word *ineluctable* on line 32, reread the line, and pick your own word to go in the blank. The word that fills the blank must be something like "unavoidable" or "certain." Which choice comes closest in meaning? Choice (C) does.

4. According to the passage, the "necessity of education" (line 34) is based in the fact that humans

   (A) have mothers and fathers
   (B) have larger brains than any other animal
   (C) are more advanced than other animals
   (D) are mortal
   (E) are born unable to feed themselves

Reread line 34 in context to see what the passage says. It states that "the primary ineluctable facts of the birth and death of each one of the constituent members in a social group determine the necessity of education." Which choice is the best paraphrase of this line? Because humans are born and die—that is, because they are mortal—explains the necessity of education. So the answer is (D).

5. The author implies, in the last paragraph, that without a concerted effort to educate the young, humans

   (A) will become extinct
   (B) may return to a more savage lifestyle
   (C) would not be as happy as those with education
   (D) will become more like stones
   (E) may have poorly behaved children

In the very last line of the passage, the author claims that "unless pains are taken to see that genuine and thorough transmission takes place, the most civilized group will relapse into barbarism and then into savagery." What choice paraphrases this line? (B) does.

Vocab Time

Turn to page 133 and memorize the Hit Parade Words for Step 10.

THE PRINCETON REVIEW
HIT PARADE

The Hit Parade is a list of the most commonly tested words on the SAT. We can't guarantee that any of them will be on your SAT, but there's a good chance that there will be a few. Moreover, these words are typical of the kind of words that appear on the SAT. By learning these words, you'll be more alert to other words of the same type when you read a book or the newspaper.

Some people like using flash cards to learn vocabulary. If this works for you, do so. Another great way to learn words is to take a few words every day and use them at every opportunity. If, for instance, you're walking down the street with your friend and you come across a flower in a garden, say, "My, what an aesthetically pleasing plant." You will probably annoy your friends, but you will certainly learn these words.

In addition to learning these words, try to read as much as you can. While you're reading, note the words you don't know and look them up in a dictionary.

STEP 1

clarity	clearness in thought or expression
cogent	convincing; reasonable
cohesive	condition of sticking together
compelling	forceful; urgently demanding attention
convoluted	intricate; complex
didactic	intended to instruct
dogmatic	characterized by a stubborn adherence to a belief
effusive	describing unrestrained emotional expression; pouring freely
emphatic	expressed or expressing with emphasis
florid	very flowery in style
fluid	easily flowing
hackneyed	overfamiliar through overuse; trite
rapport	a relationship of mutual trust or affinity
adage	a wise old saying
poignant	profoundly moving; touching
abstruse	hard to understand
arduous	difficult; strenuous
futile	serving no useful purpose
heinous	hatefully evil; abominable
impede	to slow the progress of, to interfere with
impenetrable	incapable of being penetrated; inaccessible

dilatory	tending to cause delay
enervate	to weaken the strength or vitality of
indolent	lazy
listless	lacking energy
sedentary	not migratory; involving much sitting; settled
soporific	causing sleep or sleepiness
stupor	a state of reduced or suspended sensibility
torpor	laziness; inactivity; dullness
paucity	an extreme lack of
ebullience	lively or enthusiastic expression
farce	a ridiculous or empty show
frenetic	frenzied or crazed
garrulous	given to excessive, rambling talk
gratuitous	given freely; unearned; unwarranted
insipid	uninteresting; unchallenging
ponderous	of great weight; dull
sonorous	having or producing sound; imposing or impressive
squalor	a filthy condition or quality
superfluous	extra; unnecessary
specious	having the ring of truth or plausibility but actually being false
slander	false charges and malicious oral statements or reports about someone
ruse	a crafty trick
egregious	conspicuously bad or offensive

facetious	playfully humorous
pander	to cater to the tastes and desires of others or exploit their weaknesses
propriety	appropriateness of behavior
wry	dryly humorous, often with a touch of irony
lampoon	(*n*) a broad satirical piece; (*v*) to broadly satire
parody	an artistic work that imitates the style of another work for comic effect

STEP 3

abdicate	to formally give up power
annihilate	to destroy completely
benevolent	kind; generous
despotic	characterized by exercising absolute power
dictatorial	domineering; oppressively overbearing
haughty	condescendingly proud
imperious	marked by arrogant assurance
omnipotent	all-powerful
patronizing	treating in a condescending manner
usurp	to take power by force
adamant	unyielding or inflexible
assiduous	hardworking
conscientious	careful and principled
diligent	marked by painstaking effort; hardworking
dogged	stubbornly persevering
exemplary	commendable; deserving imitation
fastidious	possessing careful attention to detail
intrepid	courageous; fearless

meticulous	extremely careful and precise
obstinate	stubbornly adhering to an opinion or a course of action
tenacity	persistent adherence to a belief or a point of view
milk	to draw or extract profit or advantage from
zealous	passionate; extremely interested in pursuing something
punctilious	strictly attentive to minute details; picky

STEP 4

alleviate	to ease a pain or a burden; to make more bearable
asylum	a place of retreat or security
auspicious	attended by favorable circumstances
benign	kind and gentle
emollient	softening and soothing
mitigate	to make less severe or painful
mollify	to calm or soothe
sanction	(v) to give official authorization or approval to
substantiated	supported with proof or evidence; verified
exculpate	to free from guilt or blame
debunk	to expose the falseness of
deleterious	having a harmful effect; injurious
disingenuous	not straightforward; crafty
disparate	fundamentally distinct or different
fabricated	made up; concocted in order to deceive
recalcitrant	defiant of authority; stubborn; not easily managed

spurious	not genuine; false
capricious	impulsive and unpredictable
disdain	feelings of contempt for others; to look down on others
glower	to look or stare angrily or sullenly
pejorative	describing words or phrases that belittle or speak negatively of someone
plagiarism	the act of passing off as one's own the ideas or writings of another
trite	unoriginal; overused; stale
vacuous	devoid of matter; empty
vilify	to lower in estimation or importance; to slander
disparage	to speak of in a slighting way or negatively; to belittle

STEP 5

aberration	a deviation from the way things normally happen or are done
dubious	doubtful; of doubtful outcome
ostentatious	describing a showy or pretentious display
quandary	a state of uncertainty or perplexity
stymied	thwarted; stumped; blocked
wily	cunning
aesthetic	having to do with beauty
decorous	proper; marked by good taste
embellish	to make beautiful by ornamenting; to add details to in order to make more attractive
idyllic	simple and carefree
medley	an assortment or a mixture, especially of musical pieces

mural	a big painting applied directly to a wall
opulent	exhibiting a display of great wealth
ornate	elaborately ornamented
pristine	not spoiled; pure
serene	calm
lucid	clear to the understanding; sane
affable	easygoing; friendly
amenable	responsive; agreeable
amiable	good-natured and likable
camaraderie	goodwill between friends
cordial	warm and sincere; friendly
gregarious	enjoying the company of others; sociable; outgoing
salutary	promoting good health
sanguine	cheerfully confident; optimistic
innocuous	having no bad effect; harmless

STEP 6

brusque	describing a rudely abrupt manner
cantankerous	grumpy; disagreeable
caustic	bitingly sarcastic or witty
contemptuous	feeling hatred; scornful; despising
feral	savage, fierce, or untamed
fractious	quarrelsome; unruly
incorrigible	unable to be reformed
ingrate	an ungrateful person
insolent	insulting in manner or speech; rude

malevolent	having or exhibiting ill will; wishing harm to others; hateful; evil
notorious	known widely and unfavorably; infamous
obdurate	stubborn; inflexible; stubbornly persisting in wrongdoing
repugnant	causing disgust or hatred
unpalatable	not pleasing to the taste
parsimonious	frugal to the point of stinginess
itinerant	traveling from place to place
remote	located far away; secluded
transitory	short-lived or temporary
unfettered	free from restrictions or bonds
harbinger	one that indicates what is to come; a forerunner
ominous	menacing; threatening
portend	to serve as an omen or a warning of
prophetic	foretelling or predicting future events
impromptu	not planned in advance; spur of the moment

STEP 7

ambiguous	open to more than one interpretation; not clear
ambivalent	simultaneously feeling opposing feelings, such as love and hate
arbiter	a judge who decides a disputed issue
inconsequential	unimportant
ample	describing an adequate or more-than-adequate amount of something
burgeoning	expanding or growing
capacious	roomy; spacious

copious	plentiful; large in quantity
permeated	spread throughout; to pass through the pores of
prodigious	enormous; exciting amazement or wonder
replete	abundantly supplied; filled
candor	sincerity; openness; frankness
frank	open and sincere in expression; straightforward, candid
pragmatic	practical
purist	one who is particularly concerned with maintaining traditional practices
terse	brief and to the point; concise
insightful	perceptive
curtailed	cut short; abbreviated
arid	describing a dry, rainless climate
conflagration	a widespread fire
nocturnal	of or occurring in the night
temperate	moderate; mild

STEP 8

clandestine	secretive, especially in regards to concealing an illicit purpose
coup	a brilliant and sudden overthrow of a government
enmity	mutual hatred or ill will
heresy	an opinion that disagrees with established, dearly held beliefs
implacable	impossible to appease or satisfy
maverick	one who is independent and resists adherence to a group

mercurial	quick and changeable in mood
pugnacious	combative; belligerent; quarrelsome
rancorous	hateful; marked by deep seated ill will
stratagem	a clever trick used to deceive or outwit
wary	on guard; watchful
thwart	to prevent the occurrence of; to successfully oppose
reclamation	a restoration or rehabilitation to productivity or usefulness; the process of reclaiming
furtive	characterized by stealth; sneaky
impetuous	characterized by sudden energy or emotion; impulsive
catalog	(*v*) to make an itemized list of
equanimity	the quality of being calm and even-tempered; composure
feasible	capable of being accomplished; possible
apt	suitable; appropriate
solvent	able to pay one's debts
facile	done or achieved with little effort; easy
liquid	flowing readily
plausible	seemingly valid or acceptable; credible; believable
biased	prejudiced
incontrovertible	indisputable; not open to question
jurisprudence	the philosophy or science of law
vindicated	freed from blame
penitent	expressing remorse for one's misdeeds

STEP 9

incumbent	(*adj*) imposed as a duty; obligatory
indigenous	originating and living in a particular area
innate	possessed at birth; inborn
inveterate	long established; deep-rooted; habitual
parochial	narrow in scope; of or relating to a church parish
pervasive	having the quality or tendency to be everywhere at the same time
impinge	to have an effect or make an impression
laconic	using few words; concise
lament	to express grief for; mourn
obsolete	no longer in use; old-fashioned
reticent	reluctant to speak
sanction	(*n*) an economic or military measure put in place to punish another country
suppressed	subdued; kept from being circulated
surreptitious	done by secretive means
truncated	shortened; cut off
wane	to decrease gradually in intensity; decline
ephemeral	lasting for a markedly brief time; fleeting
obscure	(*adj*) relatively unknown; (*v*) to conceal or make indistinct
tacit	implied but not actually expressed
tenuous	having little substance or strength; shaky; flimsy
timorous	shy; timid
trepidation	uncertainty; apprehension
immutable	not able to be changed

mundane	commonplace; ordinary
prosaic	unimaginative; dull

STEP 10

prudent	exercising good judgment or common sense
tenet	a principle held as being true by a person or an organization
stoic	indifferent to pleasure or pain; impassive
austere	somber, stern, unadorned and simple
genre	describing a category of artistic endeavor; characterized by style, content, or form
staid	characterized by a strait-laced sense of propriety; serious
archaic	characteristic of an earlier, more primitive period; old-fashioned
emulate	to try to equal through imitation
naïve	lacking sophistication
nascent	coming into existence; emerging
novice	a beginner
toxic	poisonous
brittle	easily broken, cracked, or snapped when subjected to pressure
malice	extreme ill will or spite
malfeasance	misconduct or wrongdoing, especially by a public official
dilettante	a dabbler; one who superficially understands an art or a field of knowledge
eclectic	made up of a variety of sources or styles

intuitive	known or perceived by intuition
laudatory	expressing great praise
novel	strikingly new, unusual, or different
paramount	supreme, dominant, superior to all others
urbane	notably polite and elegant in manner; suave
epiphany	a sudden burst of understanding or discovery
trenchant	keen; incisive
whimsical	subject to erratic behavior; unpredictable; acting on a whim

PART **II**

PRACTICE PROBLEMS
WITH EXPLANATIONS

The following drills will allow you to reinforce and refine the techniques you have learned in this book. If you have the time, we highly recommend that you take a few real practice SATs under timed conditions. This will give you the best possible practice, and help you prepare yourself mentally and physically for the actual test. The best book of such tests is *10 Real SATs*, published by the College Entrance Examination Board and ETS. You should be able to find it at any large bookstore or online.

DEFINITIONS

2. Which of the following is equal to the product of two consecutive integers?

    (A) 55
    (B) 56
    (C) 57
    (D) 58
    (E) 59

2. If $y \neq 0$, then $(y^3)^2 \div y^2 =$

    (A) 1
    (B) y^2
    (C) y^3
    (D) y^4
    (E) y^6

5. A rectangle with length 10 and width 4 has an area that is twice the area of a triangle with base 2. What is the height of the triangle?

    (A) 10
    (B) 15
    (C) 20
    (D) 30
    (E) 40

6. If $s = 4$, then $2s^2 + (2s)^2 =$

    (A) 32
    (B) 64
    (C) 96
    (D) 108
    (E) 128

2. **B** To get a product of about 50, the two consecutive numbers would need to be between 6 and 9. Try some consecutive integers and see what you get. $6 \times 7 = 42$, which is too small. $7 \times 8 = 56$, which is choice (B).

2. **D** $(y^3)^2$ is the same thing as y^6, so the original equation $(y^3)^2 \div y^2$ is the same thing as $\frac{y^6}{y^2}$, which reduces to y^4. Therefore the answer is (D).

5. **C** The area of the rectangle is $b \times h$, so its area is $10 \times 4 = 40$. If the area of the triangle is half of 40, this means that $\frac{1}{2}(b \times h) = 20$. You know that the base is 2, so we can solve for h, which must equal 20. Therefore the answer is (C).

6. **C** If you substitute 4 for s, the equation reads $2(4)^2 + (2 \times 4)^2$. Multiply this out, and you get $32 + 64$, which is 96—choice (C).

11. 60% of 80 is the same as 40% of what number?

   (A) 100
   (B) 105
   (C) 110
   (D) 120
   (E) 140

13. If r is a prime number greater than 2, which of the following is NOT a factor of $4r$?

   (A) r
   (B) r^2
   (C) $2r$
   (D) $4r$
   (E) 4

14. If the average of x, y, and z is 28 and the average of x and y is 12, what is the value of z?

   (A) 14
   (B) 28
   (C) 42
   (D) 60
   (E) 84

11. **D**   60% of 80 translates to $\dfrac{60}{100} \times 80$, which is the same as 48. So the problem now reads: 48 is the same as 40% of what number? You can translate this question to $48 = \dfrac{40}{100} x$. Then, you can solve for x, which equals 120; choice (D).

13. **B**   Probably the best way to approach this question is by Plugging In. Pick a prime number greater than 2 to be the value of r. Use $r = 3$. Using this number for r, the question becomes: Which of the following is NOT a factor of 12? Answer choices (A) through (E) become 3, 9, 6, 12, and 4, respectively. Which is not a factor of 12? Choice (B).

14. **D**   Because average $= \dfrac{\text{total}}{\text{number}}$ and the average of x, y, and z is 28, you know that $28 = \dfrac{x+y+z}{3}$. You don't know what x, y, and z are individually, but you know that $x + y + z = 84$. Likewise, because the average of x and y is 12, you know that $x + y = 24$. The value of z must be the difference between 84 and 24, or 60. The correct answer is (D).

PLUGGING IN

4. What is the least of four consecutive
   integers whose sum is 22?

   (A) 3
   (B) 4
   (C) 5
   (D) 6
   (E) 7

8. If $3^{x+2} = 81$, what is the value of x?

   (A) 1
   (B) 2
   (C) 3
   (D) 4
   (E) 5

14. The width of a rectangle is twice its
    height. If the perimeter of the rectangle is
    48, what is its height?

    (A) 8
    (B) 10
    (C) 12
    (D) 18
    (E) 24

4. **B** Begin by plugging in the middle answer choice, 5. If 5 is the least of four consecutive integers, the integers would be 5, 6, 7, and 8. The sum of these numbers is 26, which is too large. So try choice (B). If 4 is the least of the numbers, the numbers would be 4, 5, 6, and 7. The sum of these number is 22. So the answer is (B).

8. **B** Start with the middle choice, and assume that x is 3. Is $3^5 = 81$? No, it's larger than 81. So try choice (B), and plug in 2 for x. Is $3^4 = 81$? Yes. So the answer is (B).

14. **A** Start with choice (C) and plug in 12 for the height of the rectangle. If the width of the rectangle is twice the height, then the width must be 24. The perimeter will be 12 + 24 + 12 + 24, or 72. Choice (C) is not right. Try choice (B), and plug in 10 for the height. If the height is 10, the width must be 20, and the perimeter becomes 10 + 20 + 10 + 20, or 60. This result is still too big. So the answer must be (A). Try it to be sure. If the height is 8, the width is 16, and the perimeter is 8 + 16 + 8 + 16, which is 48.

15. John and Tim together weigh 230 pounds. If John's weight is 20 pounds more than twice Tim's weight, what is Tim's weight in pounds?

    (A) 40
    (B) 50
    (C) 60
    (D) 70
    (E) 80

16. What is the lowest possible integer for which 30 percent of that integer is greater than 1.5?

    (A) 2
    (B) 3
    (C) 5
    (D) 6
    (E) 7

17. The sum of the integers r and s is 186. The units digit of r is 5. If r is divided by 5, the result is equal to s. What is the value of r?

    (A) 55
    (B) 60
    (C) 90
    (D) 95
    (E) 155

15. **D** Begin by plugging in choice (C), or 60, for Tim's weight. If John weighs 20 pounds more than twice Tim's weight, John must weigh 20 + 2(60) = 140, and together they would weigh 200 pounds. But you know that together they should weigh 230 pounds. So (C) is too small. Try choice (D). If Tim weighs 70 pounds, then John would weigh 20 + 2(70) = 160 pounds. And, indeed, John and Tim together would weigh 230 pounds. So the answer is (D).

16. **D** Start with choice (C). Is 30% of 5 greater than 1.5? $\frac{30}{100} \times 5$ is equal to 1.5, but not greater than 1.5; therefore, (C) is too small; the answer must be (D).

17. **E** In this case, don't forget to use common sense: The problem says that the units digit of r is 5, so choices (B) and (C) can be eliminated right away. Try choice (D), and plug in 95 for r. The problem states that s is equal to r divided by 5. Because you're plugging in 95 for r, that means that $s = 19$, and that $r + s = 114$. But $r + s$ should equal 186. So (D) is too small. Try (E). When we plug in 155 for r, s becomes 31. Is 155 + 31 = 186? Yes, and the answer is (E).

PLUGGING IN YOUR OWN NUMBERS

5. If x is an odd integer greater than 1, what is the next greater odd integer in terms of x?

    (A) $x + 1$
    (B) $x + 2$
    (C) $x - 2$
    (D) $2x + 1$
    (E) $2x - 1$

6. If $t \neq 0$, then $= \dfrac{\frac{1}{8}}{2t} =$

    (A) $\dfrac{1}{8}t$

    (B) $\dfrac{4}{t}$

    (C) $\dfrac{t}{4}$

    (D) $2t$

    (E) $4t$

7. The cost of four shirts is d dollars. At this rate, what is the cost, in cents, of sixteen shirts?

    (A) $4d$

    (B) $16d$

    (C) $\dfrac{100d}{16}$

    (D) $400d$

    (E) $1,600d$

5. **B**   Plug in 3 for x. Now the question reads: What is the next greater odd integer? It's 5. Which choice says 5? (B) does.

6. **C**   Plug in 2 for t. Now the problem reads: $\dfrac{\frac{1}{8}}{2(2)}$ which is the same as $\dfrac{\frac{1}{8}}{4}$ or $\dfrac{1}{2}$. Which choice says $\dfrac{1}{2}$? (C) does.

7. **D**   Plug in a nice round number like 5 for d. If four shirts cost 5 dollars, then sixteen shirts cost 20 dollars. But the problem asks for the answer in cents. 20 dollars is the same as 2,000 cents. Which choice says 2,000 when you plug in your numbers? (D) does.

13. If a is b more than three times c, what is b in terms of a and c?

(A) $a + \frac{1}{3}c$

(B) $a + 3c$

(C) $a - \frac{1}{3}c$

(D) $a - 3c$

(E) $\frac{a - c}{2}$

16. If the sum of three consecutive integers is y, then, in terms of y, what is the least of these integers?

(A) $\frac{y}{3}$

(B) $\frac{y - 1}{3}$

(C) $\frac{y - 2}{3}$

(D) $\frac{y - 3}{3}$

(E) $\frac{y - 4}{3}$

20. If x is an odd integer and $4^x = y$, which of the following equals $16y$ in terms of x?

(A) 4^x

(B) $4^{x + 2}$

(C) 4^{2x}

(D) 4^{x2}

(E) 16^x

13. **D**   Plug in numbers for a, b, and c that obey the rule in the problem that $a = b + 3(c)$. How about 10, 4, and 2 for a, b, and c, respectively. This obeys the rule, because $10 = 4 + 3(2)$. Now the question asks "What is b?" The answer is 4. Which choice says 4? (D) does.

16. **D**   Plug in a number for y that's the sum of three consecutive integers. Because $4 + 5 + 6 = 15$, you can pick 15 for y. Now the question asks: What is the least of these integers? Plugging your numbers in, the answer is 4. Which of the choices says 4? (D) does.

20. **B**   Plug in some numbers for x and y that obey the rule that $4^x = y$. One set you could pick would be 3 and 64, because $4^3 = 64$. Now the question asks: Which of the following equals $16y$? Because our y is 64, the question asks: Which of the following is equal to 16×64, or 1,024? Which choice equals 1,024? (B) does.

GEOMETRY

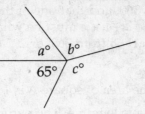

3. In the figure above, what is the value of
   $a + b + c$?

   (A) 115
   (B) 125
   (C) 235
   (D) 295
   (E) 305

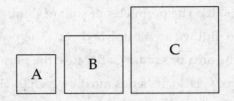

9. In the figure above, the perimeter of square
   A is $\dfrac{2}{3}$ the perimeter of square B, and the
   perimeter of square B is of the perimeter
   of square C. If the area of square A is 16,
   what is the area of square C?

   (A) 24
   (B) 36
   (C) 64
   (D) 72
   (E) 81

3. **D** In this case, all you know is that the degrees must add up to 360, and that one of the angles measures 65 degrees. So $a + b + c$ must be whatever is left when you subtract 65 from 360, or 295 degrees. The answer is (D).

9. **E** Because the area of square A is 16, you know that its sides all have length 4. The perimeter of square A is therefore also 16. We know that the perimeter of square A is $\frac{2}{3}$ the perimeter of square B, so we can calculate the perimeter of square B to be $16 = \frac{2}{3}B$. The perimeter of square B must therefore be 24. Likewise, the perimeter of square B is $\frac{2}{3}$ the perimeter of square C, so you can calculate the perimeter of square C by $24 = \frac{2}{3}C$. The perimeter of square C must therefore be 36. But we aren't finished yet! The problem asks for the area of square C. Because the perimeter of square C is 36, its sides must be each 9. The area of square C is therefore $9 \times 9 = 81$. The answer is (E).

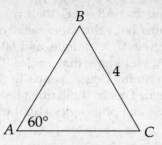

Note: Figure not drawn to scale

11. In the figure above, if $AB = AC$, then
   $AB =$

   (A) 2
   (B) 4
   (C) $2\sqrt{2}$
   (D) $2\sqrt{3}$
   (E) $4\sqrt{3}$

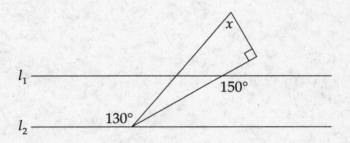

13. If l_1 is parallel to l_2 in the figure above, what is the value of x?

   (A) 20
   (B) 50
   (C) 70
   (D) 80
   (E) 90

11. **B** If you know that $AB = AC$, then we know that angles B and C must have the same measure. Because there are 180 degrees in a triangle, and 60 of them make up angle A, you know that angles B and C must split the 120 remaining degrees equally, and measure 60 degrees each. This triangle must be an equilateral triangle, with all of its sides equal to 4. The answer is (B).

13. **C** Don't forget to use POE! We know that x could not be as small as 20 degrees or as big as 90 degrees, so you can eliminate choices (A) and (E). Because l_1 is parallel to l_2, you know that 130 degrees plus the other angle in the triangle must equal 150 degrees. You can determine that the bottom angle is 20 degrees, which means that x is 70 degrees.

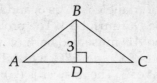

12. The area of triangle *DBC* is 6. If *AD* = *DC*, what is the area of triangle *ABC*?

(A) 4

(B) 6

(C) 12

(D) 18

(E) 24

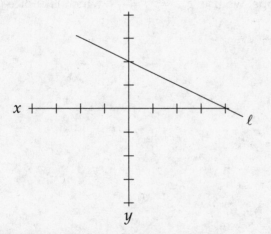

15. What is the slope of line shown in the figure above?

(A) –2

(B) $-\frac{1}{2}$

(C) 0

(D) $\frac{1}{2}$

(E) 2

12. **C**   If the area of triangle *DBC* is 6, and its height is 3, then its base *DC* must be 4. The problem says that *AD* = *DC*, so *AD* must also be 4. Now you can solve for the area of triangle *ABC*, which has a base of 8 and a height of 3. The answer is (C).

15. **B**   Don't forget to eliminate first! The line must have a negative slope, so you can eliminate choices (C), (D), and (E). If nothing else, you have a 50 percent chance of a correct answer. The two points at which the line touches the axes are at (4,0) and (0,2). To calculate slope, we use $\frac{\text{rise}}{\text{run}} = \frac{2}{-4} = -\frac{1}{2}$ which is choice (B).

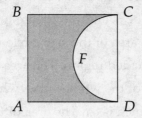

16. If *ABCD* is a square and *CFD* is a semi-circular arc with radius 4, what is the area of the shaded region?

(A) $16 - 8\pi$

(B) $16 - 8\pi$

(C) $64 - 8\pi$

(D) $64 - 16\pi$

(E) 64

16. **C**   If the radius of the semicircle is 4, then the side of the square must be 8, and the square has an area of 64. 64 minus the area of the semicircle will give us the area of the shaded region. The area of the semicircle is half the area of the whole circle, which has radius 4, or $\frac{1}{2}\pi(4)^2$, which is 8π. The area of the shaded region is therefore $64 - 8\pi$, or choice (C).

QUANTITATIVE COMPARISON

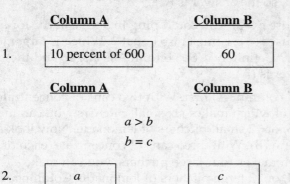

	Column A	Column B
1.	10 percent of 600	60

Column A   **Column B**

$$a > b$$
$$b = c$$

	Column A	Column B
2.	a	c

Column A   **Column B**

One can of lemonade concentrate makes
four large pitchers of lemonade or six
small pitchers of lemonade

3.	The maximum number of small pitchers of lemonade that can be made with two cans of concentrate	The maximum number of large pitchers of lemonade that can be made with three cans of concentrate

1. **C**   10% of 600 is .1 × 600, or 60. Columns A and B are equal, so the answer is (C).

2. **A**   Because $a > b$, you could plug in 3 for a and 2 for b. Because $b = c$, c must also equal 2. Which is larger, a or c? Definitely a. So column A is larger, and the answer is (A).

3. **C**   Read column (A) first. With two cans of concentrate, each of which makes six small pitchers, you can make 2 × 6, or 12 small pitchers of lemonade. Now look at column (B). With three cans of concentrate, each of which makes four large pitchers, you can make 3 × 4, or 12 large pitchers of lemonade. Columns A and B are equal, so the answer is (C).

Column A   **Column B**

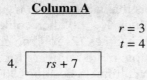

$r = 3$
$t = 4$

4. | $rs + 7$ | | $r(t + s)$ |

Column A   **Column B**

5. | The length of a side of an equilateral triangle whose perimeter is 15 | The length of a side of a triangle whose perimeter is 15 |

Column A   **Column B**

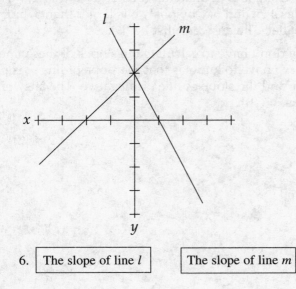

6. | The slope of line l | | The slope of line m |

4. **B**   The problem never tells us the value of s, so try plugging in a few different values. If $s = 0$, then column A becomes 7 and column B becomes 12. You can cross out (A) and (C). Try a couple more numbers for s just to be sure. If $s = 100$, then column A becomes 307 and column B becomes 312. If $s = -100$, column A becomes -293 and column B becomes -288. In every case, column B is larger. So the answer is (B).

5. **D**   You know that column A is equal to 5. Column B, however, could equal 5 (if the triangle in question is also equilateral); but column B does not specify that the triangle is equilateral. It could be a triangle with sides 4, 5, and 6. Obviously 6 is larger than 5, but 4 is smaller. The answer must be (D).

6. **B**   You don't have to calculate the slopes of these lines; all we have to know is that the slope of line m is positive and the slope of line l is negative. The answer must be (B).

	Column A	**Column B**
	$b > 2$	
7.	$\dfrac{b}{b-2}$	2

	Column A	**Column B**
Three times a equals 6 more than a.		
8.	a	3

	Column A	**Column B**
9.	$4x + 5$	$3x + 5$

7. **D**   Plug in some numbers for b. If you plug in 3 for b, then column A becomes 3, which is bigger than column B. So you can cross off choices (B) and (C). If b is 10, however, then column A becomes $\frac{10}{8}$, which is smaller than column B. Therefore the answer is (D).

8. **C**   What kind of number could a be in this problem? The only number that obeys the rule is 3, so column A equals 3, and so does column B. The answer is (C).

9. **D**   Be careful here! It may seem that column A is always larger than column B. Certainly if $x = 1$, then column A is larger. But what if $x = 0$? Then both column A and column B are equal to 5. And if $x = -1$, then column B is larger. The answer is (D).

Column A	**Column B**

$$x > 0$$

11. | $\sqrt{\dfrac{x+2}{x+2}}$ | $\sqrt{\dfrac{x}{x}} + \sqrt{\dfrac{2}{2}}$ |
|---|---|

Column A	**Column B**

s is 30 percent of *r*.

12. | $6r$ | $20s$ |
|---|---|

Column A	**Column B**

Point *P* is the center of circle *P*.
Point *Q* is the center of circle *Q*.

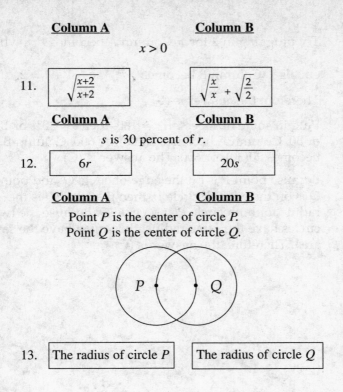

13. | The radius of circle *P* | The radius of circle *Q* |
|---|---|

11. **B**   Try plugging in 2 for x. Column A becomes $\sqrt{\frac{4}{4}}$, which

          equals 1. Column B becomes $\sqrt{\frac{2}{2}} + \sqrt{\frac{2}{2}} = 1 + 1 = 2$.

          Therefore the answer is (B).

12 **C**   Plug in some numbers. If $r = 100$, then $s = 30\%$ of 100, or 30. Column A becomes 6(100), or 600. Column B becomes 20(30), or 600. The answer is (C).

13. **C**   Because point P is on the edge of circle Q, and point Q is on the edge of circle P, then the line PQ is the radius for both circle P and circle Q. Because the two circles have the same radius, they must have the same area. Therefore, the answer is (C).

SENTENCE COMPLETIONS

1. Although he is usually very ——— at such occasions, John was surprisingly quiet at his engagement party.

    (A) reserved
    (B) outgoing
    (C) successful
    (D) irreverent
    (E) vague

2. Although a certain number of people loved Isabel's new play, it never achieved the ——— success necessary for a long run in theaters.

    (A) intellectual
    (B) eccentric
    (C) persuasive
    (D) dignified
    (E) popular

3. Unfortunately, many of Aristotle's works are ——— to us, since they were ——— along with the ancient library at Alexandria.

    (A) unknown . . promoted
    (B) lost . . destroyed
    (C) meaningless . . investigated
    (D) important . . chastised
    (E) clear . . suppressed

1. **B**   The trigger word *though* combined with the clue *surprisingly quiet* tells us that the word in the blank must be a word that means the opposite of *quiet*. The best choice is (B).

2. **E**   The trigger word *although* combined with *a certain number of people loved Isabel's play* tells us that there were not enough people who loved her play to make it a success. The word in the blank must be a word that means *widespread*. The best choice is (E).

3. **B**   Solve this problem one blank at a time. The word *unfortunately* tells us that the word in the first blank must have a negative connotation such as *lost*. This will eliminate choices (D) and (E), but at this point, (A), (B), and (C) are still possible. Now look at the second blank. The second blank must contain a word like *ruined*. Of the choices that are left, (B) is the best.

4. The team captain is an extremely
———— man; he inevitably tries to take all
the credit for his team's victories.

(A) composed
(B) plentiful
(C) egoistic
(D) cooperative
(E) articulate

5. The ———— water made it extremely
difficult for the divers to search for the
sunken treasure.

(A) transparent
(B) malodorous
(C) hazardous
(D) turbulent
(E) sparkling

6. Despite early election results that
predicted his defeat, Senator Thomas
remained ———— that he would win
the day.

(A) doubtful
(B) ignorant
(C) amicable
(D) philanthropic
(E) confident

4. **C**   The clue in this sentence is *he inevitably tries to take all the credit for his team's victories.* The word in the blank must be a word that describes such a person. The best choice is therefore (C).

5. **D**   The clue in this sentence is *made it extremely difficult for the divers to search.* What might describe water that makes it difficult to search? Perhaps a word like *murky* or *choppy.* The only choice that comes close is choice (D).

6. **E**   The trigger word *despite* combined with the clue *early election results that predicted his defeat* means that the word in the blank must be a word like *certain* or *convinced.* The only close choice is (E).

7. Despite their very ———— cultural and religious backgrounds, the leaders of the civil rights march were able to put their differences behind them and fight for a ———— goal.

(A) diverse . . common
(B) different . . poetic
(C) similar . . joint
(D) indifferent . . impossible
(E) incompatible . . remote

8. Unlike her father, who never missed an opportunity to praise the works of Charles Dickens, Amy thought that *A Tale of Two Cities* was————.

(A) excessive
(B) mediocre
(C) ingenious
(D) ambiguous
(E) anecdotal

9. The company president was not a very ———— person; he would constantly dream up projects that were impossible to carry out.

(A) radical
(B) pragmatic
(C) meticulous
(D) suspenseful
(E) inflammatory

10. She was a very ———— student; she checked every reference in her papers and always used the correct form in her footnotes.

(A) prodigious
(B) supercilious
(C) punctilious
(D) acute
(E) inspirational

7. **A**   Start with the second blank. The clue for the second blank is *were able to put their differences behind them*. What kind of word might describe such a goal? A word that means *cooperative* or *combined*. So you can eliminate (B), (D), and (E). Now look at the first blank. The trigger word *despite* means that the word in the blank must be the opposite of *cooperative* or *combined*. The best answer is (A).

8. **B**   The clue in this sentence is *Unlike her father, who never missed an opportunity to praise*. So you know that Amy does not like Dickens. Even if you can't think of your own word for the blank, you know it must be a negative word, so you can eliminate (C), (D), and (E) and you have at least a 50% chance of picking the correct answer. The best answer (and the most negative of the five choices) is (B).

9. **B**   The clue in this sentence is *would constantly dream up projects that were impossible to carry out.* Such a person is not very realistic or practical. The best answer is (B).

10. **C**   The clue in this sentence is *she checked every reference in her papers and always used the correct form in her footnotes*. What kind of word describes such a person? Careful, or a good worker. The choices in this question are all hard words, but by elimination you should be able to take a good guess. The best answer is (C).

ANALOGIES

11. LOUDSPEAKER : SOUND

(A) stem : flower
(B) lamp : light
(C) group : people
(D) year : days
(E) height : atmosphere

11. HOUR : TIME

(A) kilogram : scale
(B) length : yardstick
(C) meter : unit
(D) index : encyclopedia
(E) mile : distance

12. LID : CONTAINER

(A) part : toy
(B) dam : water
(C) roof : house
(D) dog : puppy
(E) maple : tree

12. OIL : LUBRICATE

(A) thermometer : cure
(B) antidote : poison
(C) message : transmit
(D) boat : swim
(E) ornament : decorate

11. **B** A *loudspeaker* produces *sound*. Does a *stem* produce a *flower*? No. Does a *lamp* produce *light*? Yes. Does a *group* produce *people*? No. Does a *year* produce *days*? No. Does a *height* produce *atmosphere*? No. The answer must be (B).

11. **E** An *hour* is a measure of *time*. Is a *kilogram* a measure of *scale*? No. Is a *length* a measure of a *yardstick*? No. Is a *meter* a measure of a *unit*? Sounds strange. Is an *index* the measure of an *encyclopedia*? No. Is a *mile* a measure of *distance*? Absolutely. Therefore the answer is (E).

12. **C** A *lid* is the top of a *container*. Is a *part* the top of a *toy*? No. Is a *dam* the top of *water*? No. Is the *roof* the top of a *house*? Yes. Is a *dog* the top of a *puppy*? No. Is a *maple* the top of a *tree*? No. The answer must be (C).

12. **E** *Oil* is used to *lubricate*. Is a *thermometer* used to *cure*? Maybe, but that's not really what a thermometer is. Is an *antidote* used to *poison*? Just the opposite. Is a *message* used to *transmit*? Not really; a message is something that gets transmitted. Is a *boat* used to *swim*? No. Is an *ornament* used to *decorate*? Yes. The answer is (E).

13. VACCINE : INFECTION
    (A) guard : prison
    (B) vault : theft
    (C) army : war
    (D) alcohol : intoxication
    (E) antiseptic : cleanliness

14. JUBILATION : HAPPINESS
    (A) mine : force
    (B) unity : disagreement
    (C) decency : trickery
    (D) agony : pain
    (E) hallway : light

15. RUDE : TACT
    (A) treacherous : loyalty
    (B) transparent : sight
    (C) naïve : innocence
    (D) regretful : memory
    (E) sympathetic : compassion

16. EMACIATED : THIN
    (A) audacious : bold
    (B) humid : foggy
    (C) courageous : benevolent
    (D) radiant : subtle
    (E) pathetic : contrite

13. **B**   A *vaccine* protects someone against *infection*. Does a *guard* protect against a *prison*? No. Does a *vault* protect against *theft*? Yes. Does an *army* protect against *war*? Maybe, but it also fights in a war. Does *alcohol* protect against *intoxication*? No. Does an *antiseptic* guard against *cleanliness*? Just the opposite. The answer is (B).

14. **D**   *Jubilation* means a great deal of *happiness*. If you aren't sure of the word *jubilation*, start by crossing off unrelated pairs. There is no relation between *mine* and *force*, *hallway* and *light*. Of the choices that are left— (B), (C), and (D)—choices (B) and (C) are opposite sides of the fence, and choice (D) has words that are on the same side of the fence. If you know that *jubilation* is close in meaning to *happiness*, and that *agony* means a lot of *pain*, you'll pick the correct choice: choice (D).

15. **A**   To be *rude* means to lack *tact*. Does *treacherous* mean lacking *loyalty*? Yes. Does *transparent* mean lacking *sight*? No. Does *naïve* mean lacking *innocence*? No. Does *regretful* mean lacking *memory*? No. Does *sympathetic* mean lacking *compassion*? Certainly not—it means to have compassion. Therefore, the answer is (A).

16. **A**   *Emaciated* means extremely *thin*. Does *audacious* mean very *bold*? Yes. (If you're not certain, don't eliminate it!) The other choices contain unrelated words. There is no relation between *humid* and *foggy*, *courageous* and *benevolent*, *radiant* and *subtle*, *pathetic* and *contrite*. Therefore, the answer is (A).

18. GARBLED : CLARITY
    (A) priceless : value
    (B) shallow : depth
    (C) displaced : immigrant
    (D) copied : reproduction
    (E) soft : texture

19. SOPORIFIC : SLEEP
    (A) magnet : levitation
    (B) filter : contamination
    (C) fertilizer : growth
    (D) chronograph : time
    (E) barometer : temperature

20. CAPACIOUS : VOLUME
    (A) pale : color
    (B) precious : value
    (C) muffled : noise
    (D) servile : bureaucrat
    (E) garish : shape

21. DIGRESS : SUBJECT
    (A) portray : ruse
    (B) speculate : gold
    (C) depict : character
    (D) monitor : health
    (E) stray : path

18. **B** Try Working Backward here. Choices (C), (D), and (E) are all unrelated, and can be eliminated. Only (A) and (B) make good sentences. *Garbled* means lacking in *clarity*. (If you weren't sure of the exact meaning of the words, try using Side of the Fence. *Garbled* and *clarity* have opposite meanings.) Does *priceless* mean lacking in *value*? Just the opposite. Does *shallow* mean lacking in *depth*? Yes. The correct answer is (B).

19. **C** Try Working Backward here, too. Choices (A) and (E) have unrelated words, and can be eliminated. A *filter* removes *contamination*, *fertilizer* causes *growth*, and a *chronograph* measures *time*. Which of these sentences best fits *soporific* and *sleep*? Choice (C), because a *soporific* causes *sleep*.

20. **B** Again, use Working Backward. Choices (D) and (E) contain unrelated words and can be eliminated. Can you make sentences from (A), (B), and (C)? *Pale* means lacking in *color*; *precious* means having tremendous *value*; *muffled* means a dampened or reduced *noise*. Which of these sentences works best with *capacious* and *volume*? In fact, *capacious* means having a large *volume*. Therefore the answer is (B).

21. **E** This is a hard analogy. But you can probably tell that choices (A) and (D) have no relation, and eliminate them. Then, take your best guess from the remaining choices. To *digress* means to lose track of the *subject* (of a discussion). To *stray* means to lose track of the *path*. The correct answer is (E).

CRITICAL READING

Questions 1–6 are based on the following passage.

The following passage is an excerpt from a book by novelist Gregor von Rezzori.

Skushno is a Russian word that is difficult to translate. It
means more than dreary boredom: a spiritual void that
sucks you in like a vague but intensely urgent longing.
When I was thirteen, at a phase that educators used to call
5   the awkward age, my parents were at their wits' end. We
lived in the Bukovina, today an almost astronomically
remote province in southeastern Europe. The story I am
telling seems as distant—not only in space but also in
time—as if I'd merely dreamed it. Yet it begins as a very
10 ordinary story.

I had been expelled by a *consilium abeundi*—an advisory
board with authority to expel unworthy students—from the
schools of the then Kingdom of Rumania, whose subjects
we had become upon the collapse of the Austro-Hungarian
15 Empire after the first great war. An attempt to harmonize the imbalances in my character by means of strict
discipline at a boarding school in Styria (my people still
regarded Austria as our cultural homeland) nearly led to
the same ignominious end, and only my pseudo-voluntary
20 departure from the institution in the nick of time prevented
my final ostracism from the privileged ranks of those for
whom the path to higher education was open. Again in
the jargon of those assigned the responsible task of raising children to become "useful members of society," I
25 was a "virtually hopeless case." My parents, blind to how
the contradictions within me had grown out of the highly
charged indifference between their own natures, agreed
with the schoolmasters; the mix of neurotic sensitivity
and a tendency to violence, alert perception and inability
30 to learn, tender need for support and lack of adjustability,
would only develop into something criminal.

One of the trivial aphorisms my generation owes to Wilhelm Busch's *Pious Helene* is the homily "Once your reputation's done/You can live a life of fun." But this

35   optimistic notion results more from wishful thinking than from practical experience. In my case, had anyone asked me about my state of mind, I should have sighed and answered, "*Skushno!*" Even though rebellious thoughts occasionally surged within me, I dragged myself, or

40   rather I let myself be dragged, listlessly through my bleak existence in the snail's pace of days. Nor was I ever free of a sense of guilt, for my feeling guilty was not entirely foisted upon me by others; there were deep reasons I could not explain to myself; had I been able to do so, my life

45   would have been much easier.

1. It can be inferred from the passage that the author's parents were

    (A) frustrated by their son's inability to do well in school
    (B) oblivious to their son's poor academic performance
    (C) wealthy and insensitive to the needs of the poor
    (D) schoolmasters who believed in strict discipline
    (E) happy to live apart from their son

2. Lines 15–22 are used by the author to demonstrate that

    (A) the author was an unhappy and dangerous person
    (B) the schools that the author attended were too difficult
    (C) the tactics being used to make the author more stable were failing
    (D) the author was not well-accepted by his classmates
    (E) the author's academic career was nearing an end

3. The word "ignominious" in line 19 means

    (A) dangerous
    (B) pitiless
    (C) unappreciated
    (D) disgraceful
    (E) honorable

1. **A**   Use the lead word *parents* to guide you back to the passage. Where are the author's parents discussed? At the end of the second paragraph. In these lines, the passage says that his parents agreed with the schoolmasters that he was a virtually hopeless case. The best paraphrase of this idea is (A).

2. **C**   Carefully reread these lines. The passage states that the attempt to harmonize the imbalances in his character by means of strict discipline at a boarding school in Styria nearly led to the same ignominious end. The best paraphrase of this idea is (C).

3. **D**   Cover up the word *ignominious* and put your own word in the blank. The word should mean something like "very unhappy" or "embarrassing." The choice that best fits this is (D).

4. In line 21, the word "ostracism" most likely means

   (A) praise
   (B) abuse
   (C) appreciation
   (D) departure
   (E) banishment

5. The passage as a whole suggests that the author felt

   (A) happy because he was separated from his parents
   (B) upset because he was unable to maintain good friends
   (C) melancholy and unsettled in his environment
   (D) suicidal and desperate from living in Russia
   (E) hopeful because he would soon be finished with school

6. The passage indicates that the author regarded the aphorism mentioned in the last paragraph with

   (A) relief because it showed him that he would eventually feel better
   (B) disdain because the author found it unrealistic
   (C) contempt because he saw it working for others
   (D) bemusement because of his immunity to it
   (E) sorrow because his faith in it nearly killed him

4. **E**   Cover up the word *ostracism* and put your own word in the blank. The word should mean something like "thrown out" or "exiled." The choice that best fits this is (E).

5. **C**   You know that the author is generally unhappy, so you can eliminate (A) and (E). (D) is extreme, however, and should also be eliminated. Because the author never mentions his friends, you can eliminate (B), and the best answer is (C).

6. **B**   Reread the aphorism in context. Immediately following the aphorism, the author states that this optimistic notion results more from wishful thinking than from practical experience. The best paraphrase of this idea is (B).

Questions 1–8 are based on the following passages.

In Passage 1, the author presents his view of the early years of the silent film industry. In Passage 2, the author draws on her experiences as a mime to generalize about her art.

Passage 1

Talk to those people who first saw films when they were silent, and they will tell you that the experience was magic. The silent film had extraordinary powers to draw members of an audience into the story, and an equally potent capacity

5   to make their imaginations work. It required the audience to become engaged—to supply voices and sound effects. The audience was the final, creative contributor to the process of making a film.

The finest films of the silent era depended on two elements

10   that we can seldom provide today—a large and receptive audience and a well-orchestrated score. For the audience, the fusion of picture and live music added up to more than the sum of the respective parts.

The one word that sums up the attitude of the silent film-

15   makers is enthusiasm, conveyed most strongly before formulas took shape and when there was more room for experimentation. This enthusiastic uncertainty often resulted in such accidental discoveries as new camera or editing techniques. Some films experimented with players; the 1915

20   film *Regeneration*, for example, by using real gangsters and streetwalkers, provided startling local color. Other films, particularly those of Thomas Ince, provided tragic endings as often as films by other companies supplied happy ones.

Unfortunately, the vast majority of silent films survive

25   today in inferior prints that no longer reflect the care that the original technicians put into them. The modern versions of silent films may appear jerky and flickery, but the vast picture palaces did not attract four to six thousand people a night by giving them eyestrain. A silent film

30   depends on its visuals; as soon as you degrade those, you lose elements that go far beyond the image on the surface. The acting in silents was often very subtle, very restrained, despite legends to the contrary.   Practice Problems with Explanations • **183**

Passage 2

Mime opens up a new world to the beholder, but it does so insidiously, not by purposely injecting points of interest in the manner of a tour guide. Audiences are not unlike visitors to a foreign land who discover that the modes, man-
5   ners, and thoughts of its inhabitants are not meaningless oddities, but are sensible in context.

I remember once when an audience seemed perplexed at what I was doing. At first, I tried to gain a more immediate response by using slight exaggerations. I soon realized
10 that these actions had nothing to do with the audience's understanding of the character. What I had believed to be a failure of the audience to respond in the manner I expected was, in fact, only their concentration on what I was doing; they were enjoying a gradual awakening—a
15 slow transference of their understanding from their own time and place to one that appeared so unexpectedly before their eyes. This was evidenced by their growing response to succeeding numbers.

Mime is an elusive art, as its expression is entirely depen-
20 dent on the ability of the performer to imagine a character and to re-create that character for each performance. As a mime, I am a physical medium, the instrument upon which the figures of my imagination play their dance of life. The individuals in my audience also have responsibilities—they
25 must be alert collaborators. They cannot sit back, mind-lessly complacent, and wait to have their emotions titillated by mesmeric music sounds or visual rhythms or acrobatic feats, or by words that tell them what to think. Mime is an art that, paradoxically, appeals both to those who respond
30 instinctively to entertainment and to those whose appre-ciation is more analytical and complex. Between these extremes lie those audiences conditioned to resist any col-laboration with what is played before them; and these the mime must seduce despite themselves. There is only one
35 way to attack those reluctant minds—take them unaware! They will be delighted at an unexpected pleasure.

1. Lines 11–13 of Passage 1 indicate that

    (A) music was the most important element of silent films
    (B) silent films rely on a combination of music and image in affecting an audience
    (C) the importance of music in silent film has been overestimated
    (D) live music compensated for the poor quality of silent film images
    (E) no film can succeed without a receptive audience

2. The "formulas" mentioned in line 16 of Passage 1 most probably refer to

    (A) movie theaters
    (B) use of real characters
    (C) standardized film techniques
    (D) the fusion of disparate elements
    (E) contemporary events

3. The author of Passage 1 uses the phrase "enthusiastic uncertainty" in line 17 to suggest that the filmmakers were

    (A) excited to be experimenting in an undefined area
    (B) delighted at the opportunity to study new acting formulas
    (C) optimistic in spite of the obstacles that faced them
    (D) eager to challenge existing conventions
    (E) eager to please but unsure of what the public wanted

1. **B** Go back to the passage and read lines 11–13. Just before these lines, the passage says that a well-orchestrated score was important to silent films. On lines 11-13, the passage states that for the audience, the fusion of picture and live music was important. The choice that best paraphrases this idea is (B).

2. **C** Cover up the word *formulas* and put your own word in the blank. The word should mean something that does not allow experimentation. The best choice is (C).

3. **A** According to these lines in the passage, there was a great deal of experimentation that led to such accidental discoveries as new camera or editing techniques. The choice that best paraphrases this idea is (A).

4. The word *legends* in line 33 of Passage 1
   most nearly means

   (A) fairy tales
   (B) symbolism
   (C) heroes
   (D) movie stars
   (E) misconceptions

5. The author of Passage 2 mentioned the
   incident in lines 7–13 in order to imply
   that

   (A) the audience's lack of response
       reflected their captivated interest in
       the performance
   (B) she was forced to resort to stereo-
       types in order to reach her audience
   (C) exaggeration is an essential part of
       mime
   (D) the audience had a good understand-
       ing of the subtlety of mime
   (E) vocalization is helpful in reaching
       certain audiences

6. Lines 7–13 indicate that the author of Passage
   2 and the silent filmmakers of Passage 1 were
   similar because

   (A) neither used many props
   (B) both conveyed their message by using
       sophisticated technology
   (C) both learned through trial and error
   (D) both used visual effects and dialogue
   (E) both had a loyal following

4. **E**   Cover up the word *legends* and put your own word in the blank. The word should mean something like "false opinions" or "wrong ideas." The choice that fits this is (E).

5. **A**   In lines 7–13, the author says "What I believed to be a failure of the audience to respond in the manner I expected was, in fact, only their concentration on what I was doing . . .". The choice that best paraphrases this idea is (A).

6. **C**   Reread lines 7–13. If you're stuck, use POE. Because neither props nor sophisticated technology were ever mentioned, you can eliminate (A) and (B). A loyal following is not mentioned in these lines either, so eliminate (E). Choice (D) contradicts the point of the passage, because a mime does not use dialogue. Therefore, the answer must be (C).

7. Lines 21–23 suggest that the author of Passage 2 feels that mimes

(A) cannot control the way audiences interpret their characters

(B) transform their bodies to portray their characters

(C) have to resist outside attempts to define their acting style

(D) should focus on important events in the lives of specific characters

(E) know the limitations of performances that do not incorporate either music or speech

8. Passages 1 and 2 are similar in that both are mainly concerned with

(A) the use of special effects

(B) differences among dramatic styles

(C) the visual aspects of performance

(D) the suspension of disbelief in audiences

(E) nostalgia for a bygone era

7. **B** Reread lines 21–23. These lines state that "As a mime, I am a physical medium, the instrument upon which the figures of my imagination play their dance of life." The best paraphrase of this idea is (B).

8. **C** POE is your best friend on this question. Special effects and suspension of disbelief are never mentioned, so eliminate (A) and (D). Nostalgia is not part of passage 2, so eliminate (E). If you're stuck at this point, guess! The passage never actually discusses differences among styles, so the best answer is (C).

ABOUT THE AUTHOR

Jeff Rubenstein is Senior Director of Research and Development at The Princeton Review. He has been with The Princeton Review since 1989.

NOTES

NOTES

NOTES

NOTES